ultimate
cake mix
book

Publications International, Ltd.

Favorite Brand Name Recipes at www.fbnr.com

Microwave Cooking: Microwave ovens vary in wattage. Use the cooking times as guidelines and check for doneness before adding more time.
Preparation/Cooking Times: Preparation times are based on the approximate amount of time required to assemble the recipe before cooking, baking, chilling or serving. These times include preparation steps such as measuring, chopping and mixing. The fact that some preparations and cooking can be done simultaneously is taken into account. Preparation of optional ingredients and serving suggestions is not included.

Table of Contents

Cake Mix
Classics

chocolate glazed citrus poppy seed cake

1 package (about 18 ounces) lemon cake mix
1 container (8 ounces) plain lowfat yogurt
3 eggs
$\frac{1}{3}$ cup milk
$\frac{1}{3}$ cup poppy seeds
1 teaspoon freshly grated lemon peel
   Chocolate Citrus Glaze (recipe follows)

1. Heat oven to 350°F. Grease and flour 12-cup fluted tube pan or 10-inch tube pan.

2. Combine cake mix, yogurt, eggs, milk, poppy seeds and lemon peel in large bowl; beat until well blended. Pour batter into prepared pan.

3. Bake 40 to 45 minutes or until wooden pick inserted in center comes out clean. Cool 20 minutes; remove from pan to wire rack. Cool completely.

4. Prepare Chocolate Citrus Glaze; spoon over cake, allowing glaze to run down sides.   *Makes 12 servings*

Chocolate Citrus Glaze: Melt 2 tablespoons butter or margarine in small saucepan over medium heat. Stir in 2 tablespoons HERSHEY'S Cocoa or HERSHEY'S SPECIAL DARK™ Cocoa, 2 tablespoons water, 1 tablespoon orange-flavored liqueur, if desired, and $\frac{1}{2}$ teaspoon orange extract. Whisk in $1\frac{1}{4}$ cups powdered sugar until smooth. If glaze is too thin, whisk in additional $\frac{1}{4}$ cup powdered sugar. Use immediately.

easy upside down cake

1 can (20 ounces) DOLE® Pineapple Slices
¼ cup butter or margarine, melted
⅔ cup packed brown sugar
10 maraschino cherries
1 package (18.25 ounces) yellow or pineapple-flavored cake mix

• Drain pineapple, reserving ¾ cup juice.

• Stir together melted butter and brown sugar in 12-inch skillet with heatproof handle. Arrange pineapple slices in sugar mixture. Place cherry in center of each pineapple slice.

• Prepare cake mix according to package directions, replacing water with reserved ¾ cup juice. Pour batter evenly over pineapple.

• Bake at 350°F 40 to 45 minutes or until toothpick inserted in center comes out clean.

• Cool 5 minutes. Loosen edges and invert onto serving platter.

Makes 10 servings

Note: Cake can be baked in 13×9-inch baking pan instead of skillet. Prepare and assemble cake as above except cut two pineapple slices in half and place whole slices along edges of pan and halved slices in center. Place cherries in center of slices. Bake and cool as above.

Mini Upside Down Cakes: **Drain** 1 can (20 ounces) DOLE® Crushed Pineapple, reserving juice. Grease 24 muffin cups. **Stir** ⅓ cup melted butter with ⅔ cup packed brown sugar. Evenly spoon mixture into bottoms of cups; spoon about 1 tablespoon crushed pineapple over sugar mixture. **Prepare** cake mix as above. Evenly pour batter into cups. **Bake** 20 to 25 minutes. Invert onto serving platter. Makes 24 servings.

Prep Time: 15 minutes
Bake Time: 40 minutes

Cake Mix Classics

7

pink lady cake

1 package (about 18 ounces) devil's food cake mix, plus ingredients
  to prepare mix
1 container (16 ounces) vanilla frosting
  Red food coloring
1 package (3 ounces) ladyfingers, split in half

1. Preheat oven to 350°F. Grease two 8-inch round cake pans.

2. Prepare cake mix according to package directions. Spread batter evenly
in prepared pans.

3. Bake 30 minutes or until toothpick inserted into centers comes out clean.
Cool cake layers completely in pans on wire racks.

4. Combine frosting and enough food coloring in large bowl to reach
desired shade of pink. Remove cake layers from pans. Place one layer
on serving plate; spread with ½ cup frosting. Top with second cake layer;
frost top and side of cake with remaining frosting.

5. Arrange ladyfingers around side of cake, pressing flat sides into frosting
as shown in photo. Tie ribbon around cake, if desired.

Makes 12 servings

banana fudge layer cake

1 package DUNCAN HINES® Moist Deluxe® Yellow Cake Mix
1⅓ cups water
3 eggs
⅓ cup vegetable oil
1 cup mashed ripe bananas (about 3 medium)
1 container DUNCAN HINES® Chocolate Frosting

1. Preheat oven to 350°F. Grease and flour two 9-inch round cake pans.

2. Combine cake mix, water, eggs and oil in large bowl. Beat at low speed with electric mixer until moistened. Beat at medium speed 2 minutes. Stir in bananas.

3. Pour into prepared pans. Bake at 350°F for 28 to 31 minutes or until toothpick inserted in center comes out clean. Cool in pans 15 minutes. Remove from pans; cool completely.

4. Fill and frost cake with frosting. Garnish as desired.

Makes 12 to 16 servings

To ripen bananas, store them at room temperature. To speed ripening, place them in an unsealed paper bag. Brown speckles on the skins are an indication of ripeness, and black patches means the bananas are overripe. (Overripe bananas are still good to use in baking.)

cookies 'n' cream cake

1 package (about 18 ounces) white cake mix *without* pudding
    in the mix
1 package (4-serving size) white chocolate instant pudding
    and pie filling mix
1 cup vegetable oil
4 egg whites
½ cup milk
20 chocolate sandwich cookies, coarsely chopped
½ cup semisweet chocolate chips
1 teaspoon shortening
4 chocolate sandwich cookies, cut into quarters

1. Preheat oven to 350°F. Spray 12-cup bundt pan with nonstick cooking spray.

2. Beat cake mix, pudding mix, oil, egg whites and milk in large bowl with electric mixer at medium speed 2 minutes or until ingredients are well blended. Stir in chopped cookies; spread in prepared pan.

3. Bake 50 to 60 minutes or until cake springs back when lightly touched. Cool 1 hour in pan on wire rack. Invert cake onto serving plate; cool completely.

4. Combine chocolate chips and shortening in small microwavable bowl. Microwave on HIGH 1 minute; stir. Microwave at 15-second intervals, as necessary, stirring until melted and smooth. Drizzle glaze over cake and garnish with quartered cookies. *Makes 12 servings*

elegant chocolate angel torte

⅓ cup HERSHEY₅S Cocoa
1 package (about 16 ounces) angel food cake mix
2 envelopes (1.3 ounces each) dry whipped topping mix
1 cup cold nonfat milk
1 teaspoon vanilla extract
1 cup strawberry purée*
   Strawberries

*Mash 2 cups sliced fresh strawberries (or frozen berries, thawed) in blender or food processor. Cover; blend until smooth. Purée should measure 1 cup.

1. Move oven rack to lowest position.

2. Sift cocoa over dry cake mix in large bowl; stir to blend. Proceed with mixing cake as directed on package. Bake and cool as directed for 10-inch tube pan. Carefully run knife along side of pan to loosen cake; remove from pan. Using serrated knife, slice cake horizontally into four layers.

3. Prepare whipped topping mix as directed on package, using 1 cup nonfat milk and 1 teaspoon vanilla. Fold in strawberry purée.

4. Place bottom cake layer on serving plate; spread with ¼ of strawberry topping. Set next cake layer on top; spread with ¼ of topping. Continue layering cake and topping. Garnish with strawberries. Refrigerate until ready to serve. Slice cake with sharp serrated knife, cutting with gentle sawing motion. Cover; refrigerate leftover cake.   *Makes about 16 servings*

Prep Time: 30 minutes
Bake Time: 45 minutes
Cool Time: 2 hours

coconut lemon torte

1 (14-ounce) can **EAGLE BRAND**® **Sweetened Condensed Milk**
    (NOT evaporated milk)
2 **egg yolks**
½ **cup lemon juice**
1 **teaspoon grated lemon rind (optional)**
    Yellow food coloring (optional)
1 **(18.25- or 18.5-ounce) package white cake mix**
1 **(4-ounce) container frozen nondairy whipped topping, thawed**
    (1¾ cups)
    Flaked coconut

1. In medium saucepan, combine EAGLE BRAND®, egg yolks, lemon juice, lemon rind (optional) and food coloring (optional). Over medium heat, cook and stir until slightly thickened, about 10 minutes. Chill.

2. Preheat oven to 350°F. Grease and flour two 9-inch round cake pans. Prepare cake mix as package directs. Pour batter into prepared pans. Bake 30 minutes or until lightly browned. Remove from pans; cool completely.

3. With sharp knife, remove crust from top of each cake layer. Split layers horizontally. Spread equal portions of lemon mixture between layers and on top to within 1 inch of edge.

4. Frost side and 1-inch rim on top of cake with whipped topping. Coat side of cake with coconut; garnish as desired. Store leftovers covered in refrigerator. *Makes one (9-inch) cake*

delicate white chocolate cake

1 package **DUNCAN HINES®** Moist Deluxe® White Cake Mix
1 package (4-serving size) vanilla-flavor instant pudding and
     pie filling mix
4 egg whites
1 cup water
½ cup vegetable oil
5 ounces finely chopped white chocolate
1 cup cherry preserves
8 drops red food coloring (optional)
2 cups whipping cream, chilled
2 tablespoons confectioners' sugar
   Maraschino cherries for garnish
1 ounce white chocolate shavings for garnish

1. Preheat oven to 350°F. Cut waxed paper circles to fit bottoms of three
9-inch round cake pans. Grease bottoms and sides of pans. Line with
waxed paper circles.

2. Combine cake mix, pudding mix, egg whites, water and oil in large
mixing bowl. Beat at medium speed with electric mixer for 2 minutes.
Fold in chopped white chocolate. Pour into prepared pans. Bake at 350°F
for 18 to 22 minutes or until toothpick inserted in center comes out clean.
Cool in pans 15 minutes. Invert onto cooling racks. Peel off waxed paper.
Cool completely.

3. Combine cherry preserves and food coloring, if desired. Stir to blend
color.

4. Beat whipping cream in large bowl until soft peaks form. Add sugar
gradually. Beat until stiff peaks form.

continued on page 20

5. To assemble, place one cake layer on serving plate. Spread ½ cup cherry preserves over cake. Place second cake layer on top. Spread with remaining preserves. Place third cake layer on top. Frost side and top of cake with whipped cream. Decorate with maraschino cherries and white chocolate shavings. Refrigerate until ready to serve.

Makes 12 to 16 servings

butterscotch bundt cake

1 package (about 18 ounces) yellow cake mix *without* pudding
   in the mix
1 package (4-serving size) butterscotch instant pudding and
   pie filling mix
1 cup water
3 eggs
2 teaspoons ground cinnamon
½ cup chopped pecans
   Powdered sugar (optional)

1. Preheat oven to 325°F. Spray 12-cup bundt pan with nonstick cooking spray.

2. Beat cake mix, pudding mix, water, eggs and cinnamon in large bowl with electric mixer at medium-high speed 2 minutes or until blended. Stir in pecans. Pour into prepared pan.

3. Bake 40 to 50 minutes or until cake springs back when lightly touched. Cool in pan on wire rack 10 minutes. Invert cake onto serving plate; cool completely. Sprinkle with powdered sugar.   *Makes 12 to 16 servings*

Pistachio Walnut Bundt Cake: Substitute white cake mix for yellow cake mix, pistachio pudding mix for butterscotch pudding mix and walnuts for pecans.

candy bar cake

1 package (about 18 ounces) devil's food cake mix *without* pudding in the mix

1 cup sour cream

4 eggs

⅓ cup vegetable oil

¼ cup water

3 containers (16 ounces each) white frosting

1 bar (2.1 ounces) chocolate-covered crispy peanut butter candy, chopped

1 bar (2.07 ounces) chocolate-covered peanut, caramel and nougat candy, chopped

1 bar (1.4 ounces) chocolate-covered toffee candy, chopped

4 bars (1.55 ounces each) milk chocolate

1. Preheat oven to 350°F. Grease and flour two 9-inch round cake pans.

2. Beat cake mix, sour cream, eggs, oil and water in large bowl with electric mixer at low speed about 1 minute or until blended. Increase speed to medium; beat 1 to 2 minutes or until smooth. Spread batter in prepared pans.

3. Bake 30 to 35 minutes or until toothpick inserted into center comes out clean. Cool cake layers in pans 10 minutes. Remove from pans; cool completely on wire racks.

4. Cut each cake layer in half horizontally. Place one cake layer on serving plate. Spread generously with frosting. Sprinkle with one chopped candy bar. Repeat with two more cake layers, additional frosting and remaining two chopped candy bars. Top with remaining cake layer; frost top of cake with remaining frosting.

5. Break milk chocolate bars into pieces along score lines. Stand chocolate pieces in frosting around outside edge of cake.   *Makes 12 servings*

almond cake

1 can (8 ounces) almond paste
3 eggs
1 package (about 18 ounces) white cake mix
1¼ cups water
⅓ cup vegetable oil
1 cup seedless raspberry preserves
1 container (12 ounces) whipped vanilla frosting
Candy-coated almonds

1. Preheat oven to 350°F. Grease two 9-inch round cake pans.

2. Combine almond paste and eggs in large bowl; stir until completely smooth. Add cake mix, water and oil; beat with electric mixer at low speed 1 minute. Beat at medium-low speed 2 minutes or until well blended. Pour batter into prepared pans.

3. Bake 35 minutes or until toothpick inserted into centers comes out clean. Cool completely in pans on wire racks.

4. Remove cake layers from pans. Place one layer on serving plate; spread with preserves to within ¼ inch of edge. Top with remaining cake layer. Frost top and side of cake with frosting. Decorate with almonds.

Makes 12 servings

carrot layer cake

Cake

 1 package DUNCAN HINES® Moist Deluxe® Classic Yellow Cake Mix
 4 eggs
 ½ cup vegetable oil
 3 cups grated carrots
 1 cup finely chopped nuts
 2 teaspoons ground cinnamon

Cream Cheese Frosting

 1 package (8 ounces) cream cheese, softened
 ¼ cup (½ stick) butter or margarine, softened
 2 teaspoons vanilla extract
 4 cups confectioners' sugar

1. Preheat oven to 350°F. Grease and flour two 8- or 9-inch round baking pans.

2. For cake, combine cake mix, eggs, oil, carrots, nuts and cinnamon in large bowl. Beat at low speed with electric mixer until moistened. Beat at medium speed for 2 minutes. Pour into prepared pans. Bake at 350°F for 35 to 40 minutes or until toothpick inserted into centers comes out clean. Cool.

3. For cream cheese frosting, place cream cheese, butter and vanilla extract in large bowl. Beat at low speed until smooth and creamy. Add confectioners' sugar gradually, beating until smooth. Add more sugar to thicken, or milk or water to thin frosting, as needed. Fill and frost cooled cake. Garnish with whole pecans.   *Makes 12 to 16 servings*

german upside-down cake

1½ cups shredded coconut
1 cup pecan pieces
1 container (16 ounces) coconut pecan frosting
1 package (about 18 ounces) German chocolate cake mix
1⅓ cups water
4 eggs
1 cup milk chocolate chips
⅓ cup vegetable oil
   Whipped cream (optional)

1. Preheat oven to 350°F. Spray 13×9-inch glass baking dish with nonstick cooking spray.

2. Spread coconut evenly in prepared pan. Sprinkle pecans over coconut. Spoon frosting by tablespoonfuls over pecans. (Do not spread.)

3. Beat cake mix, water, eggs, chocolate chips and oil in large bowl with electric mixer at low speed 30 seconds. Beat at medium speed 2 minutes or until well blended and creamy. Pour batter into prepared pan, spreading carefully over frosting.

4. Bake 35 to 40 minutes or until toothpick inserted into center comes out clean. Cool in pan 10 minutes; invert onto serving plate. Serve warm; top with whipped cream, if desired. *Makes 16 to 18 servings*

fudgy ripple cake

1 package (18.25 ounces) yellow cake mix, plus ingredients
    to prepare mix
1 package (3 ounces) cream cheese, softened
2 tablespoons unsweetened cocoa powder
    Fudgy Glaze (recipe follows)
½ cup "M&M's"® Chocolate Mini Baking Bits

Preheat oven to 350°F. Lightly grease and flour 10-inch bundt or ring pan; set aside. Prepare cake mix as package directs. In medium bowl combine 1½ cups prepared batter, cream cheese and cocoa powder until smooth. Pour half of yellow batter into prepared pan. Drop spoonfuls of chocolate batter over yellow batter in pan. Top with remaining yellow batter. Bake about 45 minutes or until toothpick inserted near center comes out clean. Cool completely on wire rack. Unmold cake onto serving plate. Prepare Fudgy Glaze; spread over top of cake, allowing some glaze to run over side. Sprinkle with "M&M's"® Chocolate Mini Baking Bits. Store in tightly covered container.   *Makes 10 servings*

Fudgy Glaze: Place 1 square (1 ounce) semi-sweet chocolate in small microwave-safe bowl. Microwave at HIGH 30 seconds; stir. Repeat as necessary until chocolate is completely melted, stirring at 10-second intervals; set aside. In medium bowl combine 1 cup powdered sugar and ⅓ cup unsweetened cocoa powder. Stir in 3 tablespoons milk, ½ teaspoon vanilla extract and melted chocolate until smooth.

red velvet cake

2 packages (about 18 ounces each) white cake mix
2 teaspoons baking soda
3 cups buttermilk
4 eggs
2 bottles (1 ounce each) red food coloring
2 containers (16 ounces each) vanilla frosting

1. Preheat oven to 350°F. Grease and flour four 9-inch round cake pans.

2. Combine cake mixes and baking soda in large bowl. Add buttermilk, eggs and food coloring; beat with electric mixer at low speed until moistened. Beat at high speed 2 minutes. Pour batter into prepared pans.

3. Bake 30 to 35 minutes or until toothpick inserted into centers comes out clean. Cool cake layers in pans 10 minutes. Remove from pans; cool completely on wire racks.

4. Place one cake layer on serving plate; spread with frosting. Repeat with second and third cake layers. Top with fourth cake layer; frost top and side of cake.   *Makes 16 servings*

boston cream pie

1 package DUNCAN HINES® Moist Deluxe® Classic Yellow Cake Mix
2 containers (3½ ounces each) ready-to-eat vanilla pudding
1 container DUNCAN HINES® Chocolate Frosting

1. Preheat oven to 350°F. Grease and flour two 8- or 9-inch round pans.

2. Prepare, bake and cool cakes following package directions for basic recipe.

3. To assemble, place one cake layer on serving plate. Spread contents of 2 containers of vanilla pudding on top of cake. Top with second cake layer. Remove lid and foil top of Chocolate frosting container. Heat in microwave oven at HIGH (100% power) for 25 to 30 seconds. Stir. (Mixture should be thin.) Spread chocolate glaze over top of second cake layer. Refrigerate until ready to serve. *Makes 12 to 16 servings*

For a richer flavor, substitute DUNCAN HINES® Butter Recipe Golden Cake Mix in place of Yellow Cake Mix.

Crazy for
Cupcakes

carrot cream cheese cupcakes

1 package (8 ounces) cream cheese, softened
¼ cup powdered sugar
1 package (about 18 ounces) spice cake mix, plus ingredients
    to prepare mix
2 cups grated carrots
2 tablespoons finely chopped candied ginger
1 container (16 ounces) cream cheese frosting
3 tablespoons maple syrup
   Orange peel strips (optional)

1. Preheat oven to 350°F. Line 14 jumbo (3½-inch) muffin cups with paper or foil baking cups.

2. Beat cream cheese and powdered sugar in large bowl with electric mixer at medium speed 1 minute or until light and fluffy.

3. Prepare cake mix according to package directions; stir in carrots and ginger. Fill muffin cups one-third full (about ¼ cup batter). Place 1 tablespoon cream cheese mixture in center of each cup. Top with remaining batter (muffin cups should be two-thirds full).

4. Bake 25 to 28 minutes or until toothpick inserted into centers comes out clean. Cool cupcakes in pans 10 minutes. Remove from pans; cool completely on wire racks.

5. Mix frosting and maple syrup until well blended. Frost tops of cupcakes; decorate with orange peel. *Makes 14 cupcakes*

chocolate cherry cupcakes

1 package (about 18 ounces) devil's food cake mix *without* pudding
    in the mix
1⅓ cups water
 3 eggs
 ½ cup sour cream
 ⅓ cup vegetable oil
 1 cup dried cherries
 1 container (16 ounces) vanilla frosting, divided
    Green food coloring
11 maraschino cherries, stemmed and cut into halves

1. Preheat oven to 350°F. Line 22 standard (2½-inch) muffin cups with paper baking cups.

2. Beat cake mix, water, eggs, sour cream and oil in large bowl with electric mixer at low speed 30 seconds or until just blended. Beat at medium speed 2 minutes or until smooth. Fold in dried cherries. Spoon batter into prepared muffin cups, filling three-fourths full.

3. Bake 20 to 24 minutes or until toothpick inserted into centers comes out clean. Cool cupcakes in pans 10 minutes. Remove from pans; cool completely on wire racks.

4. Place ¼ cup frosting in small bowl; stir in food coloring, one drop at a time, until desired shade of green is reached.

5. Frost cupcakes with remaining white frosting. Place 1 cherry half, cut side down, onto each cupcake. Place green frosting in piping bag fitted with writing tip. Pipe cherry stem and leaf onto each cupcake.

Makes 22 cupcakes

surprise package cupcakes

1 package (about 18 ounces) cake mix, any flavor, plus ingredients
　　to prepare mix
1 container (16 ounces) vanilla frosting
　　Food coloring (optional)
1 tube (4¼ ounces) white decorating icing
72 chewy fruit squares
　　Colored decors

1. Preheat oven to 350°F. Spray 24 standard (2½-inch) muffin cups with nonstick cooking spray or line with paper baking cups.

2. Prepare and bake cake mix in prepared muffin cups according to package directions. Cool cupcakes in pans 15 minutes. Remove from pans; cool completely on wire racks.

3. Tint frosting with food coloring, adding a few drops at a time until desired color is reached. Spread frosting over cupcakes.

4. Use icing to pipe "ribbons" on fruit squares to resemble wrapped presents. Arrange 3 candy presents on each cupcake. Decorate with decors.   *Makes 24 cupcakes*

triple-chocolate cupcakes

1 package (18¼ ounces) chocolate cake mix
1 package (4 ounces) chocolate instant pudding and pie filling mix
1 container (8 ounces) sour cream
4 large eggs
½ cup vegetable oil
½ cup warm water
2 cups (12-ounce package) NESTLÉ® TOLL HOUSE® Semi-Sweet
   Chocolate Morsels
2 containers (16 ounces *each*) prepared frosting
   Assorted candy sprinkles

PREHEAT oven to 350°F. Grease or paper-line 30 muffin cups.

COMBINE cake mix, pudding mix, sour cream, eggs, vegetable oil and water in large mixer bowl; beat on low speed just until blended. Beat on high speed for 2 minutes. Stir in morsels. Pour into prepared muffin cups, filling two-thirds full.

BAKE for 25 to 28 minutes or until wooden pick inserted in centers comes out clean. Cool in pans for 10 minutes; remove to wire racks to cool completely. Frost; decorate with candy sprinkles.   *Makes 30 cupcakes*

If you bake cupcakes for the holidays, vary your baking cups and sprinkles to match the occasion. Use pink for Valentine's Day; red, white and blue for Independence Day; and orange and black for Halloween.

white chocolate macadamia cupcakes

1 package (about 18 ounces) white cake mix *without* pudding in
   the mix, plus ingredients to prepare mix
1 package (4-serving size) white chocolate instant pudding
   and pie filling mix
¾ cup chopped macadamia nuts
1½ cups flaked coconut
1 cup white chocolate chips
1 container (16 ounces) white frosting

1. Preheat oven to 350°F. Line 20 standard (2½-inch) muffin cups with
paper baking cups.

2. Prepare cake mix according to package directions, adding pudding
mix with cake mix ingredients. Fold in macadamia nuts. Spoon batter into
prepared muffin cups, filling two-thirds full.

3. Bake 18 to 20 minutes or until toothpick inserted into centers comes
out clean. Cool cupcakes in pans 10 minutes. Remove from pans; cool
completely on wire racks.

4. Meanwhile, spread coconut evenly on ungreased baking sheet; bake
at 350°F 6 minutes, stirring occasionally, until light golden brown. Cool
completely.

5. Place white chocolate chips in small microwavable bowl; microwave
2 minutes on MEDIUM (50%), stirring every 30 seconds, until melted and
smooth. Cool slightly; stir into frosting. Frost cupcakes; sprinkle with
toasted coconut. *Makes 20 cupcakes*

marshmallow fudge sundae cupcakes

1 package (about 18 ounces) chocolate cake mix, plus ingredients
   to prepare mix
2 packages (4 ounces each) waffle bowls
40 large marshmallows
1 jar (8 ounces) hot fudge topping
1¼ cups whipped topping
¼ cup colored sprinkles
1 jar (10 ounces) maraschino cherries

1. Preheat oven to 350°F. Lightly spray 20 standard (2½-inch) muffin cups with nonstick cooking spray.

2. Prepare cake mix according to package directions. Spoon batter into prepared muffin cups, filling two-thirds full.

3. Bake 20 minutes or until toothpick inserted into centers comes out clean. Cool cupcakes in pans on wire racks about 10 minutes.

4. Remove cupcakes from pans and place one cupcake in each waffle bowl. Place waffle bowls on baking sheets. Top each cupcake with 2 marshmallows; return to oven 2 minutes or until marshmallows are slightly softened.

5. Remove lid from fudge topping; heat in microwave on HIGH 10 seconds or until softened. Top each cupcake with 2 teaspoons fudge topping, 1 tablespoon whipped topping, sprinkles and a cherry.

Makes 20 cupcakes

boston cream cupcakes

1 package (about 18 ounces) yellow cake mix, plus ingredients
    to prepare mix
¼ cup French vanilla instant pudding and pie filling mix
1 cup cold milk
1 container (16 ounces) dark chocolate frosting

1. Preheat oven to 350°F. Lightly spray 22 standard (2½-inch) muffin cups with nonstick cooking spray.

2. Prepare and bake cake mix according to package directions for cupcakes. Cool cupcakes in pans 10 minutes. Remove from pans; cool completely on wire racks.

3. Meanwhile, whisk pudding mix and milk until well blended. Cover and refrigerate.

4. Gently poke small hole into bottom of each cupcake, using tip of knife or toothpick. Place pudding in pastry bag fitted with small round pastry tip.*

5. Place tip inside hole at bottom of cupcake; gently squeeze bag to fill cupcake with pudding. Repeat with remaining cupcakes and pudding.

6. Place frosting in medium microwavable bowl. Microwave on HIGH 30 seconds; stir. Frost tops of cupcakes. *Makes 22 cupcakes*

Or use a plastic squeeze bottle with narrow dispensing tip.

black & whites

1 package (about 18 ounces) vanilla cake mix, plus ingredients
    to prepare mix

$\frac{2}{3}$ cup semisweet chocolate chips, melted and cooled slightly

4 ounces cream cheese, softened

1 cup prepared vanilla frosting

1 cup prepared chocolate frosting

1. Preheat oven to 350°F. Line 24 standard (2½-inch) muffin cups with paper baking cups.

2. Prepare cake mix according to package directions. Reserve half of batter (about 2½ cups) in medium bowl. Add melted chocolate and cream cheese to remaining batter; beat with electric mixer at medium speed about 2 minutes or until smooth and well blended.

3. Spoon chocolate and vanilla batters side by side into prepared muffin cups, filling about two-thirds full. (Use chocolate batter first as it is slightly thicker and easier to position on one side of each muffin cup.)

4. Bake about 16 minutes or until toothpick inserted into centers comes out clean. Cool cupcakes in pans 10 minutes. Remove from pans; cool completely on wire racks.

5. Spread vanilla frosting over half of each cupcake; spread chocolate frosting over remaining half of each cupcake. *Makes 24 cupcakes*

caramel apple cupcakes

1 package (about 18 ounces) butter or yellow cake mix,
plus ingredients to prepare mix
1 cup chopped dried apples
Caramel Frosting (recipe follows)
Chopped nuts (optional)

1. Preheat oven to 375°F. Line 24 standard (2½-inch) muffin cups with paper baking cups.

2. Prepare cake mix according to package directions; stir in apples. Spoon batter into prepared muffin cups, filling two-thirds full.

3. Bake 15 to 20 minutes or until toothpick inserted into centers comes out clean. Cool cupcakes in pans 10 minutes. Remove from pans; cool completely on wire racks.

4. Prepare Caramel Frosting. Frost cupcakes; sprinkle with nuts.

Makes 24 cupcakes

Caramel Frosting: Melt 3 tablespoons butter in small saucepan. Stir in 1 cup packed light brown sugar, ½ cup evaporated milk and ⅛ teaspoon salt. Bring to a boil, stirring constantly. Remove from heat; cool slightly. Add 3¾ cups powdered sugar; beat until frosting is spreading consistency. Add ¾ teaspoon vanilla; beat until smooth.

iced coffee cupcakes

1 package (about 18 ounces) chocolate fudge cake mix *without* pudding in the mix
1 package (4-serving size) chocolate instant pudding mix
1⅓ cups brewed coffee, cooled to room temperature
3 eggs
½ cup vegetable oil
1 teaspoon vanilla
½ gallon mocha almond fudge or coffee ice cream, softened
1 bottle (7¼ ounces) quick-hardening chocolate shell dessert topping
½ cup pecan pieces, toasted

1. Preheat oven to 350°F. Line 20 standard (2½-inch) muffin cups with foil baking cups or spray with nonstick cooking spray.

2. Beat cake mix, pudding mix, coffee, eggs, oil and vanilla in large bowl with electric mixer at low speed 30 seconds. Beat at medium speed 2 minutes or until well blended and fluffy. Spoon into prepared muffin cups, filling three-fourths full.

3. Bake 15 to 20 minutes or until toothpick inserted into centers comes out clean. Cool cupcakes in pans 10 minutes. Remove from pans; cool completely on wire racks.

4. Working one at a time, remove 1 tablespoon cake from center of each cupcake top. Fill depression with 2 to 3 tablespoons ice cream, mounding on top. Spoon about 1 tablespoon dessert topping over ice cream; quickly sprinkle with pecans before topping hardens. Place cupcakes in freezer until ready to serve.

Makes 20 cupcakes

ice cream cone cupcakes

1 package (about 18 ounces) white cake mix, plus ingredients
to prepare mix
2 tablespoons nonpareils
24 flat-bottomed ice cream cones
Prepared vanilla and chocolate frostings
Additional nonpareils and decors

1. Preheat oven to 350°F.

2. Prepare cake mix according to package directions; stir in nonpareils. Stand cones in 13×9-inch baking pan or muffin cups. Spoon ¼ cup batter into each ice cream cone.

3. Bake about 20 minutes or until toothpicks inserted into centers come out clean. Cool completely on wire racks.

4. Frost cupcakes and decorate as desired.   *Makes 24 cupcakes*

These cupcakes are best served the day they are prepared. If it is necessary to store them, cover them loosely.

lemon-up cakes

1 package (about 18 ounces) butter recipe white cake mix with pudding in the mix, plus ingredients to prepare mix

$\frac{1}{2}$ cup lemon juice, divided (2 large lemons)

Grated peel of 2 lemons, divided

$\frac{1}{2}$ cup (1 stick) butter, softened

$3\frac{1}{2}$ cups powdered sugar

Yellow food coloring

1 package ($9\frac{1}{2}$ ounces) lemon-shaped hard candies, coarsely crushed

1. Preheat oven to 350°F. Spray 24 standard (2½-inch) muffin cups with nonstick cooking spray or line with paper baking cups.

2. Prepare cake mix according to package directions but use ¼ cup less water than directions call for. Stir in ¼ cup lemon juice and half of grated lemon peel. Spoon batter evenly into prepared muffin cups.

3. Bake 23 minutes or until light golden brown and toothpick inserted into centers comes out clean. Cool cupcakes in pans 5 minutes. Remove from pans; cool completely on wire racks.

4. Beat butter in large bowl with electric mixer at medium speed until creamy. Gradually add powdered sugar. Add remaining ¼ cup lemon juice, lemon peel and several drops food coloring; beat at high speed until frosting is light and fluffy.

5. Frost cupcakes; sprinkle with crushed candies.

Makes 24 cupcakes

cappuccino cupcakes

1 package (about 18 ounces) dark chocolate cake mix
$1\frac{1}{3}$ cups strong brewed or instant coffee, at room temperature
3 eggs
$\frac{1}{3}$ cup vegetable oil or melted butter
1 container (16 ounces) vanilla frosting
2 tablespoons coffee liqueur
Additional coffee liqueur (optional)
Grated chocolate*
Chocolate-covered coffee beans (optional)

*Grate half of a 3- or 4-ounce milk, dark or espresso chocolate candy bar on the large holes of a grater.

1. Preheat oven to 350°F. Line 24 standard (2½-inch) muffin cups with foil or paper baking cups.

2. Beat cake mix, coffee, eggs and oil in large bowl with electric mixer at low speed 30 seconds. Beat at medium speed 2 minutes. Spoon batter into prepared muffin cups, filling two-thirds full.

3. Bake 18 to 20 minutes or until toothpick inserted into centers comes out clean. Cool cupcakes in pans 10 minutes. Remove from pans; cool completely on wire racks. (At this point, cupcakes may be frozen for up to 3 months. Thaw at room temperature before frosting.)

4. Combine frosting and 2 tablespoons liqueur in small bowl; mix well. Before frosting, poke about 10 holes in each cupcake with toothpick. Pour 1 to 2 teaspoons liqueur over top of each cupcake, if desired. Frost and sprinkle with grated chocolate. Garnish with chocolate-covered coffee beans, if desired.

Makes 24 cupcakes

banana split cupcakes

1 package (about 18 ounces) yellow cake mix, divided
1 cup water
1 cup mashed ripe bananas
3 eggs
1 cup chopped drained maraschino cherries
1½ cups mini semisweet chocolate chips, divided
1½ cups prepared vanilla frosting
1 cup marshmallow creme
1 teaspoon shortening
30 whole maraschino cherries, drained and patted dry

1. Preheat oven to 350°F. Line 30 standard (2½-inch) muffin cups with paper baking cups.

2. Reserve 2 tablespoons cake mix. Beat remaining cake mix, water, bananas and eggs in large bowl with electric mixer at low speed about 30 seconds or until moistened. Beat at medium speed 2 minutes. Combine chopped cherries and reserved cake mix in small bowl. Stir chopped cherry mixture and 1 cup chocolate chips into batter. Spoon batter into prepared muffin cups, filling two-thirds full.

3. Bake 15 to 20 minutes or until toothpick inserted into centers comes out clean. Cool cupcakes in pans 10 minutes. Remove from pans; cool completely on wire racks.

4. Combine frosting and marshmallow creme in medium bowl until well blended. Frost cupcakes.

5. Combine remaining ½ cup chocolate chips and shortening in small microwavable bowl. Microwave on HIGH 30 to 45 seconds, stirring after 30 seconds, or until smooth. Drizzle chocolate mixture over cupcakes. Place one whole cherry on each cupcake. *Makes 30 cupcakes*

Variation: If desired, omit chocolate drizzle and top cupcakes with colored sprinkles.

mini doughnut cupcakes

1 cup sugar

1½ teaspoons ground cinnamon

1 package (about 18 ounces) yellow or white cake mix, plus ingredients to prepare mix

1 tablespoon ground nutmeg

1. Preheat oven to 350°F. Grease and flour 48 mini (1¾-inch) muffin cups. Combine sugar and cinnamon in small bowl; set aside.

2. Prepare cake mix according to package directions; stir in nutmeg. Spoon batter into prepared muffin cups, filling two-thirds full.

3. Bake about 12 minutes or until lightly browned and toothpick inserted into centers comes out clean.

4. Remove cupcakes from pans. Roll warm cupcakes in sugar mixture until completely coated. *Makes 48 mini cupcakes*

Use a nonstick cooking spray with flour added to make preparing the pans much quicker and easier.

peanut butter & milk chocolate cupcakes

1 package (about 18 ounces) butter recipe yellow cake mix with pudding in the mix, plus ingredients to prepare mix

½ cup creamy peanut butter

¼ cup (½ stick) butter

2 bars (3½ ounces each) good-quality milk chocolate, broken into small pieces

¼ cup (½ stick) unsalted butter, cut into small chunks

¼ cup whipping cream

Dash salt

Peanut butter chips (optional)

1. Preheat oven to 350°F. Line 24 standard (2½-inch) muffin cups with paper baking cups.

2. Prepare cake mix according to package directions with ½ cup peanut butter and ¼ cup butter (instead of ½ cup butter called for in directions). Fill muffin cups evenly with batter.

3. Bake 24 to 26 minutes or until light golden brown and toothpick inserted into centers comes out clean. Cool cupcakes in pans 5 minutes. Remove from pans; cool completely on wire racks.

4. Combine chocolate, unsalted butter, cream and salt in small, heavy saucepan. Heat over very low heat, stirring constantly, just until butter and chocolate melt. Mixture should be warm, not hot. Immediately spoon about 1 tablespoon chocolate glaze over each cupcake, spreading to cover top. Sprinkle with peanut butter chips. *Makes 24 cupcakes*

Incredible
Cookies

moon rocks

1 package (about 18 ounces) devil's food or German chocolate cake
    mix with pudding in the mix
3 eggs
½ cup (1 stick) butter, melted
2 cups slightly crushed (2½-inch) pretzel sticks
1½ cups uncooked old-fashioned oats
1 cup swirled chocolate and white chocolate chips or candy-coated
    semisweet chocolate baking pieces

1. Preheat oven to 350°F.

2. Blend cake mix, eggs and butter in large bowl. Stir in pretzels, oats and
chocolate chips. (Dough will be stiff.) Drop dough by rounded teaspoonfuls
about 2 inches apart onto ungreased cookie sheets.

3. Bake 7 to 9 minutes or until set. Cool cookies on cookie sheets 1 minute;
remove to wire racks to cool completely. *Makes 5 dozen cookies*

quick fruit & lemon drops

½ cup sugar
1 package (about 18 ounces) lemon cake mix
⅓ cup water
¼ cup (½ stick) butter, softened
1 egg
1 tablespoon grated lemon peel
1 cup mixed dried fruit bits

1. Preheat oven to 350°F. Grease cookie sheets. Place sugar in shallow
bowl.

2. Beat cake mix, water, butter, egg and lemon peel in large bowl with
electric mixer at low speed until well blended. Beat in fruit bits just until

blended. Shape heaping tablespoons of dough into balls; roll in sugar to coat. Place 2 inches apart on prepared cookie sheets.

3. Bake 12 to 14 minutes or until set. Cool cookies on cookie sheets 2 minutes; remove to wire racks to cool completely.

Makes about 2 dozen cookies

Tip: If dough is too sticky to handle, add about ¼ cup all-purpose flour.

chocolate peanut butter cookies

½ cup (1 stick) butter, softened
½ cup creamy peanut butter
1 egg
2 tablespoons water
1 package (about 18 ounces) chocolate cake mix with pudding in the mix
1 package (12 ounces) semisweet chocolate chips
¼ cup creamy peanut butter
¼ cup chopped peanuts

1. Preheat oven to 350°F. Line two cookie sheets with parchment paper.

2. Beat butter and peanut butter in large bowl with electric mixer at medium speed until well blended. Add egg and water; beat until well blended. Beat in cake mix until well blended.

3. Shape level teaspoonfuls of batter into balls. Place on prepared cookie sheets; flatten to ⅓-inch thickness with bottom of glass dipped in sugar. Bake 12 to 15 minutes or until set. Cool cookies on cookie sheets 2 minutes; remove to wire racks to cool completely.

4. Melt chocolate chips and peanut butter in top of double boiler, stirring occasionally. Stir in peanuts. Spread about 1 teaspoon mixture on each cookie. Set aside 2 hours or refrigerate 1 hour to allow frosting to set.

Makes about 4 dozen cookies

coconut clouds

2⅔ cups flaked coconut, divided
1 package DUNCAN HINES® Moist Deluxe® Classic Yellow Cake Mix
1 egg
½ cup vegetable oil
¼ cup water
1 teaspoon almond extract

1. Preheat oven to 350°F. Reserve 1⅓ cups coconut in medium bowl.

2. Combine cake mix, egg, oil, water and almond extract in large bowl. Beat at low speed with electric mixer. Stir in remaining 1⅓ cups coconut. Drop rounded teaspoonful of dough into reserved coconut. Roll to cover lightly. Place on ungreased baking sheet. Repeat with remaining dough, placing balls 2 inches apart.

3. Bake at 350°F for 10 to 12 minutes or until light golden brown. Cool 1 minute on baking sheets. Remove to cooling racks. Cool completely. Store in airtight container.

Makes 3½ dozen cookies

To save time when forming dough into balls, use a 1-inch spring-operated cookie scoop. Spring-operated cookie scoops are available at kitchen specialty shops.

sweet mysteries

1 package (about 18 ounces) yellow cake mix with pudding in the mix
½ cup (1 stick) butter, softened
1 egg yolk
1 cup ground pecans
36 milk chocolate candy kisses, unwrapped
   Powdered sugar

1. Preheat oven to 300°F.

2. Beat half of cake mix and butter in large bowl with electric mixer at high speed until blended. Add egg yolk and remaining cake mix; beat at medium speed just until dough forms. Stir in pecans.

3. Shape rounded tablespoon of dough around each candy, making sure candy is completely covered. Place 1 inch apart on ungreased cookie sheets.

4. Bake 20 to 25 minutes or until firm and just beginning to turn golden. Cool cookies on cookie sheets 10 minutes. Place waxed paper under wire racks. Remove cookies to wire racks; sprinkle with powdered sugar.

Makes 3 dozen cookies

blondie biscotti with almonds

1 cup slivered almonds
1 package (about 18 ounces) white cake mix
⅔ cup all-purpose flour
2 eggs
3 tablespoons melted butter, cooled slightly
1 teaspoon vanilla
3 tablespoons grated lemon peel

1. Preheat oven to 350°F. Line cookie sheet with parchment paper.

2. Heat medium skillet over medium heat. Add almonds and cook 1½ to 2 minutes or just until fragrant, stirring constantly. *Do not brown.* Set aside.

3. Beat cake mix, flour, eggs, butter and vanilla in large bowl with electric mixer at low speed 1 to 2 minutes or until well blended. Stir in almonds and lemon peel. Knead dough 7 to 8 times or until ingredients are well blended.

4. Divide dough in half. Shape each half into 12×2×½-inch log; place logs 3 inches apart on prepared cookie sheet.

5. Bake 25 minutes or until toothpick inserted into centers of logs comes out clean. Cool on cookie sheet on wire rack 25 minutes.

6. Remove biscotti logs to cutting board, peeling off parchment paper. Cut each log diagonally into ½-inch slices with serrated knife. Place slices, cut sides down, on cookie sheet. Bake 10 minutes or until bottoms of slices are golden brown. Remove to wire racks to cool completely. Store in airtight container.

Makes about 3 dozen biscotti

garbage pail cookies

1 package (about 18 ounces) white cake mix with pudding in the mix
½ cup (1 stick) butter, softened
2 eggs
1 teaspoon ground cinnamon
1 teaspoon vanilla
½ cup peanut butter chips
½ cup salted peanuts
½ cup mini candy-coated chocolate pieces
1½ cups crushed salted potato chips

1. Preheat oven to 350°F. Lightly grease cookie sheets.

2. Beat half of cake mix, butter, eggs, cinnamon and vanilla in large bowl with electric mixer at medium speed until light. Beat in remaining cake mix until well blended. Stir in peanut butter chips, peanuts and candy-coated chocolate pieces. Stir in potato chips. (Dough will be stiff.) Drop batter by rounded tablespoonfuls 2 inches apart onto prepared cookie sheets.

3. Bake 15 minutes or until golden brown. Cool cookies on cookie sheets 2 minutes; remove to wire racks to cool completely.

Makes about 3½ dozen cookies

To soften butter quickly, place one stick of butter on a microwavable plate and heat on LOW (30%) about 30 seconds or just until softened.

crispy thumbprint cookies

1 package (about 18 ounces) yellow cake mix
½ cup vegetable oil
¼ cup water
1 egg
3 cups crisp rice cereal, crushed
½ cup chopped walnuts
6 tablespoons raspberry or strawberry preserves

1. Preheat oven to 375°F.

2. Beat cake mix, oil, water and egg in large bowl with electric mixer at medium speed until well blended. Add cereal and walnuts; beat until well blended.

3. Drop dough by heaping teaspoonfuls about 2 inches apart onto ungreased cookie sheets. Use thumb to make indentation in each cookie. Spoon about ½ teaspoon preserves into center of each cookie.

4. Bake 9 to 11 minutes or until golden brown. Cool cookies on cookie sheets 1 minute; remove to wire racks to cool completely.

Makes 3 dozen cookies

Prep and Bake Time: **30 minutes**

pinwheel cookies

½ cup shortening plus additional for greasing
⅓ cup plus 1 tablespoon butter, softened and divided
2 egg yolks
½ teaspoon vanilla extract
1 package DUNCAN HINES® Moist Deluxe® Fudge Marble Cake Mix

1. Combine ½ cup shortening, ⅓ cup butter, egg yolks and vanilla extract in large bowl. Mix at low speed with electric mixer until blended. Set aside cocoa packet from cake mix. Gradually add cake mix. Blend well.

2. Divide dough in half. Add cocoa packet and remaining 1 tablespoon butter to one half of dough. Knead until well blended and chocolate colored.

3. Roll out yellow dough between two pieces of waxed paper into 18×12×⅛-inch rectangle. Repeat with chocolate dough. Remove top pieces of waxed paper from chocolate and yellow doughs. Place yellow dough directly on top of chocolate dough. Remove remaining layers of waxed paper. Roll up jelly-roll fashion, beginning at wide side. Refrigerate 2 hours.

4. Preheat oven to 350°F. Grease baking sheets.

5. Cut dough into ⅛-inch slices. Place sliced dough 1 inch apart on prepared baking sheets. Bake at 350°F for 9 to 11 minutes or until lightly browned. Cool 5 minutes on baking sheets. Remove to cooling racks.

Makes about 3½ dozen cookies

chocolate chip-oat cookies

1 package (about 18 ounces) yellow cake mix
1 teaspoon baking powder
¾ cup vegetable oil
2 eggs
1 teaspoon vanilla
1 cup uncooked old-fashioned oats
¾ cup semisweet chocolate chips

1. Preheat oven to 350°F. Lightly grease cookie sheets or line with parchment paper.

2. Combine cake mix and baking powder in large bowl. Add oil, eggs and vanilla; beat with electric mixer at low speed 3 minutes or until well blended. Stir in oats and chocolate chips.

3. Drop dough by slightly rounded tablespoonfuls 2 inches apart onto prepared cookie sheets.

4. Bake 10 minutes or until golden brown. Cool cookies on cookie sheets 5 minutes; remove to wire racks to cool completely.

Makes 4 dozen cookies

quick chocolate softies

1 package (about 18 ounces) devil's food cake mix
1/3 cup water
1/4 cup (1/2 stick) butter, softened
1 egg
1 cup white chocolate chips
1/2 cup coarsely chopped walnuts

1. Preheat oven to 350°F. Grease cookie sheets.

2. Beat cake mix, water, butter and egg in large bowl with electric mixer at low speed until moistened. Beat at medium speed 1 minute. (Dough will be stiff.) Stir in white chocolate chips and nuts; stir until well blended. Drop dough by heaping teaspoonfuls 2 inches apart onto prepared cookie sheets.

3. Bake 10 to 12 minutes or until set. Cool cookies on cookie sheets 1 minute; remove to wire racks to cool completely.

Makes about 4 dozen cookies

If you're baking several batches of cookies using the same cookie sheets, make sure to let the cookie sheets cool to room temperature before adding more dough. Hot cookie sheets will cause the dough to melt and spread, which can result in very flat and/or overbaked cookies.

cinnamon cereal crispies

½ cup granulated sugar

2 teaspoons ground cinnamon, divided

1 package (about 18 ounces) white or yellow cake mix with pudding
   in the mix

½ cup water

⅓ cup vegetable oil

1 egg

2 cups crisp rice cereal

1 cup cornflakes

1 cup raisins

1 cup chopped nuts (optional)

1. Preheat oven to 350°F. Lightly spray cookie sheets with nonstick cooking spray. Combine sugar and 1 teaspoon cinnamon in small bowl.

2. Beat cake mix, water, oil, egg and remaining 1 teaspoon cinnamon in large bowl with electric mixer at medium speed 1 minute. Gently stir in rice cereal, cornflakes, raisins and nuts, if desired, until well blended. Drop dough by rounded tablespoonfuls 2 inches apart onto prepared cookie sheets. Sprinkle lightly with half of cinnamon-sugar mixture.

3. Bake about 15 minutes or until lightly browned. Sprinkle cookies with remaining cinnamon-sugar mixture; remove to wire racks to cool completely.   *Makes about 5 dozen cookies*

chocolate almond biscotti

1 package **DUNCAN HINES**® Moist Deluxe® Dark Chocolate Cake Mix
1 cup all-purpose flour
½ cup butter or margarine, melted
2 eggs
1 teaspoon almond extract
½ cup chopped almonds
   White chocolate, melted (optional)

1. Preheat oven to 350°F. Line 2 baking sheets with parchment paper.

2. Combine cake mix, flour, butter, eggs and almond extract in large bowl. Beat at low speed with electric mixer until well blended; stir in almonds. Divide dough in half. Shape each half into 12×2-inch log; place logs on prepared baking sheets.

3. Bake at 350°F for 30 to 35 minutes or until toothpick inserted in center comes out clean. Remove logs from oven; cool on baking sheets 15 minutes. Using serrated knife, cut logs into ½-inch slices. Arrange slices on baking sheets. Bake biscotti 10 minutes. Remove to cooling racks; cool completely.

4. Dip one end of each biscotti in melted white chocolate, if desired. Allow white chocolate to set at room temperature before storing biscotti in airtight container.   *Makes about 2½ dozen cookies*

sunshine sandwiches

$\frac{1}{3}$ cup coarse or granulated sugar
$\frac{3}{4}$ cup ($1\frac{1}{2}$ sticks) plus 2 tablespoons butter, softened, divided
1 egg
2 tablespoons grated lemon peel
1 package (about 18 ounces) lemon cake mix with pudding in the mix
$\frac{1}{4}$ cup yellow cornmeal
2 cups sifted powdered sugar
2 to 3 tablespoons lemon juice

1. Preheat oven to 375°F. Place coarse sugar in shallow bowl.

2. Beat $\frac{3}{4}$ cup butter in large bowl with electric mixer at medium speed until fluffy. Add egg and lemon peel; beat 30 seconds. Add cake mix, one third at a time, beating at low speed after each addition until combined. Stir in cornmeal. (Dough will be stiff.)

3. Shape dough into 1-inch balls; roll in sugar to coat. Place 2 inches apart on ungreased cookie sheets.

4. Bake 8 to 9 minutes or until bottoms begin to brown. Cool cookies on cookie sheets 1 minute; remove to wire racks to cool completely.

5. Meanwhile, beat powdered sugar and remaining 2 tablespoons butter in small bowl with electric mixer at low speed until blended. Gradually add enough lemon juice to reach spreading consistency.

6. Spread 1 slightly rounded teaspoon frosting on bottom of one cookie. Top with second cookie, bottom side down. Repeat with remaining cookies and frosting. Store covered at room temperature for up to 24 hours or freeze.   *Makes 1½ dozen sandwich cookies*

cranberry gems

⅔ cup dried cranberries or dried cherries
½ cup granulated sugar
3 tablespoons water, divided
1 package (about 18 ounces) white cake mix with pudding in the mix
2 eggs
2 tablespoons vegetable oil
¼ teaspoon almond extract or vanilla
½ cup powdered sugar
1 to 2 teaspoons milk

1. Preheat oven to 350°F. Lightly grease cookie sheets.

2. Combine cranberries, granulated sugar and 1 tablespoon water in small microwavable bowl. Microwave on HIGH 1 minute; let cranberries stand 10 minutes before draining.

3. Blend cake mix, eggs, remaining 2 tablespoons water, oil and almond extract in large bowl until smooth. Drop dough by rounded teaspoonfuls 2 inches apart onto prepared cookie sheets. Top each cookie with several cranberries.

4. Bake 10 minutes or until edges are lightly browned. Top each cookie with 1 or 2 additional cranberries after baking. Remove to wire racks to cool completely.

5. Blend powdered sugar and 1 teaspoon milk in small bowl until smooth. Add additional milk if necessary to reach drizzling consistency. Drizzle glaze over cookies with tip of small spoon or fork.

Makes about 5 dozen cookies

pastel mint swirls

⅓ cup coarse or granulated sugar

1 package (about 18 ounces) devil's food cake mix *without* pudding in the mix

3 eggs

¼ cup (½ stick) butter, melted

¼ cup unsweetened cocoa powder

144 small or 48 large pastel mint chips

1. Preheat oven to 375°F. Place sugar in shallow bowl.

2. Combine cake mix, eggs, butter and cocoa in large bowl just until blended. (Dough will be stiff.)

3. Shape dough into 1-inch balls; roll in sugar to coat. Place 2 inches apart on ungreased cookie sheets.

4. Bake 8 to 9 minutes or until tops are cracked. Gently press 3 small or 1 large mint into top of each cookie. Cool cookies on cookie sheets 1 minute; remove to wire racks to cool completely.

Makes 4 dozen cookies

Very Best

Bars

jam jam bars

1 package (about 18 ounces) yellow or white cake mix with pudding in the mix
½ cup (1 stick) butter, melted
1 cup apricot preserves or raspberry jam
1 package (11 ounces) peanut butter and milk chocolate chips

1. Preheat oven to 350°F. Lightly spray 13×9-inch baking pan with nonstick cooking spray.

2. Pour cake mix into large bowl; stir in melted butter until well blended. Remove ½ cup dough and set aside. Press remaining dough evenly into prepared pan. Spread preserves evenly over dough in pan.

3. Place chips in medium bowl. Stir in reserved dough until well mixed. (Dough will remain in small lumps evenly distributed throughout chips.) Sprinkle mixture evenly over preserves.

4. Bake 20 minutes or until lightly browned and bubbly at edges. Cool completely in pan on wire rack. *Makes 3 dozen bars*

buckeye cookie bars

1 (18.25- or 18.5-ounce) package chocolate cake mix
¼ cup vegetable oil
1 egg
1 cup chopped peanuts
1 (14-ounce) can EAGLE BRAND® Sweetened Condensed Milk (NOT evaporated milk)
½ cup peanut butter

1. Preheat oven to 350°F (325°F for a glass dish). In large bowl, combine cake mix, oil and egg; beat at medium speed until crumbly. Stir in peanuts. Reserve 1½ cups crumb mixture; press remaining crumb mixture firmly on bottom of greased 13×9-inch baking pan.

2. In medium bowl, beat EAGLE BRAND® with peanut butter until smooth; spread over prepared crust. Sprinkle with reserved crumb mixture.

3. Bake 25 to 30 minutes or until set. Cool. Cut into bars. Store loosely covered at room temperature.   *Makes 2 to 3 dozen bars*

Prep Time: 20 minutes
Bake Time: 25 to 30 minutes

sweet walnut maple bars

Crust

    1 package DUNCAN HINES® Moist Deluxe® Classic Yellow Cake Mix, divided

    $\frac{1}{3}$ cup butter or margarine, melted

    1 egg

Topping

    $1\frac{1}{3}$ cups MRS. BUTTERWORTH'S® Maple Syrup

    3 eggs

    $\frac{1}{3}$ cup firmly packed light brown sugar

    $\frac{1}{2}$ teaspoon maple flavoring or vanilla extract

    1 cup chopped walnuts

1. Preheat oven to 350°F. Grease 13×9×2-inch pan.

2. For crust, reserve $\frac{2}{3}$ cup cake mix; set aside. Combine remaining cake mix, melted butter and egg in large bowl. Stir until thoroughly blended. (Mixture will be crumbly.) Press into prepared pan. Bake at 350°F for 15 to 20 minutes or until light golden brown.

3. For topping, combine reserved cake mix, maple syrup, eggs, brown sugar and maple flavoring in large bowl. Beat at low speed with electric mixer for 3 minutes. Pour over crust. Sprinkle with walnuts. Bake at 350°F for 30 to 35 minutes or until filling is set. Cool completely. Cut into bars. Store leftover bars in refrigerator.   *Makes 24 bars*

Very Best Bars

buried cherry bars

1 jar (10 ounces) maraschino cherries
1 package (about 18 ounces) devil's food cake mix *without* pudding
   in the mix
1 cup (2 sticks) butter, melted
1 egg
$\frac{1}{2}$ teaspoon almond extract
$1\frac{1}{2}$ cups semisweet chocolate chips
$\frac{3}{4}$ cup sweetened condensed milk
$\frac{1}{2}$ cup chopped pecans

1. Preheat oven to 350°F. Lightly grease 13×9-inch baking pan. Drain maraschino cherries, reserving 2 tablespoons juice. Cut cherries into quarters.

2. Combine cake mix, butter, egg and almond extract in large bowl; mix well. (Batter will be very thick.) Spread batter in prepared pan. Lightly press cherries into batter.

3. Combine chocolate chips and sweetened condensed milk in small saucepan. Cook over low heat, stirring constantly, until chocolate melts. Stir in reserved cherry juice. Spread chocolate mixture over cherries in pan; sprinkle with pecans.

4. Bake 35 minutes or until almost set in center. Cool completely in pan on wire rack. Cut into triangles or squares. *Makes 2 dozen bars*

granola raisin bars

1 package (about 18 ounces) yellow cake mix with pudding in the mix,
   divided
½ cup (1 stick) butter, melted, divided
1 egg
4 cups granola cereal with raisins

1. Preheat oven to 350°F. Lightly spray 13×9-inch baking pan with nonstick cooking spray. Reserve ½ cup cake mix; set aside.

2. Combine remaining cake mix, ¼ cup melted butter and egg in large bowl; stir until well blended. (Dough will be thick and sticky.) Press dough evenly into prepared pan with plastic wrap. Bake 8 minutes.

3. Meanwhile, combine reserved cake mix, granola cereal and remaining ¼ cup melted butter in medium bowl; stir until well blended. Spread mixture evenly over partially baked bars.

4. Bake 15 to 20 minutes or until edges are lightly browned. Cool completely in pan on wire rack.

Makes 2½ dozen bars

easy turtle bars

1 package (about 18 ounces) chocolate cake mix
½ cup (1 stick) butter, melted
¼ cup milk
1 cup (6 ounces) semisweet chocolate chips
1 cup chopped pecans
1 jar (12 ounces) caramel ice cream topping

1. Preheat oven to 350°F. Spray 13×9-inch baking pan with nonstick cooking spray.

2. Combine cake mix, butter and milk in large bowl; stir until well blended. Press half of batter into prepared pan. Bake 7 to 8 minutes or until crust begins to form.

3. Sprinkle chocolate chips and half of pecans over partially baked crust. Drizzle with caramel topping. Drop spoonfuls of remaining batter over caramel mixture; sprinkle with remaining pecans.

4. Bake 18 to 20 minutes or until top springs back when lightly touched. (Caramel center will be soft.) Cool completely in pan on wire rack. Cut into bars.   *Makes 2½ dozen bars*

peanut butter cheesecake bars

1 package (about 18 ounces) yellow cake mix with pudding in the mix
$\frac{1}{2}$ cup (1 stick) butter, softened, cut into small pieces
2 packages (8 ounces each) cream cheese, softened
1 cup chunky peanut butter
3 eggs
$1\frac{1}{4}$ cups sugar
1 cup salted roasted peanuts
Melted chocolate (optional)

1. Preheat oven to 325°F.

2. Beat cake mix and butter in medium bowl with electric mixer at medium speed just until crumbly. Reserve 1 cup dough. Press remaining dough evenly into ungreased 13×9-inch baking pan to form crust. Bake 10 minutes; cool on wire rack.

3. Beat cream cheese and peanut butter in large bowl with electric mixer at medium speed until fluffy. Beat in eggs, one at a time, scraping down side of bowl occasionally. Gradually beat in sugar until light. Spoon filling over cooled crust. Combine reserved dough and peanuts; sprinkle over filling.

4. Bake 45 minutes or until filling is just set and knife inserted into center comes out clean. Cool in pan on wire rack 30 minutes. Refrigerate at least 2 hours before serving. Drizzle with melted chocolate, if desired.

Makes 2 to 3 dozen bars

lemon bars

1 package DUNCAN HINES® Moist Deluxe® Lemon Supreme Cake Mix
3 eggs, divided
⅓ cup butter-flavor shortening
½ cup granulated sugar
¼ cup lemon juice
2 teaspoons grated lemon peel
½ teaspoon baking powder
¼ teaspoon salt
Confectioners' sugar

1. Preheat oven to 350°F.

2. Combine cake mix, 1 egg and shortening in large mixing bowl. Beat at low speed with electric mixer until crumbs form. Reserve 1 cup. Pat remaining mixture lightly into *ungreased* 13×9-inch pan. Bake at 350°F for 15 minutes or until lightly browned.

3. Combine remaining 2 eggs, granulated sugar, lemon juice, lemon peel, baking powder and salt in medium mixing bowl. Beat at medium speed with electric mixer until light and foamy. Pour over hot crust. Sprinkle with reserved crumb mixture.

4. Bake at 350°F for 15 minutes or until lightly browned. Sprinkle with confectioners' sugar. Cool in pan. Cut into bars. *Makes 30 to 32 bars*

These bars are also delicious using Duncan Hines® Moist Deluxe® Classic Yellow Cake Mix.

ice cream sandwiches

1 package (about 18 ounces) chocolate cake mix with pudding in the mix

2 eggs

$\frac{1}{4}$ cup warm water

3 tablespoons butter, melted

2 cups vanilla ice cream, softened

Colored sugars or sprinkles

1. Preheat oven to 350°F. Lightly spray 13×9-inch pan with nonstick cooking spray. Line pan with foil and spray foil.

2. Beat cake mix, eggs, water and melted butter in large bowl with electric mixer until well blended. (Dough will be thick and sticky.) Press dough evenly into prepared pan; prick surface with tines of fork (about 40 times).

3. Bake 20 minutes or until toothpick inserted into center comes out clean. Cool in pan on wire rack.

4. Cut cookie in half crosswise; remove one half from pan. Spread ice cream evenly over cookie half remaining in pan. Top with second half; use foil in pan to wrap up sandwich.

5. Freeze at least 4 hours. Cut into 8 equal pieces; dip cut ends in sugar or sprinkles. Wrap sandwiches individually and freeze until ready to serve.

Makes 8 sandwiches

Peppermint Ice Cream Sandwiches: Stir $\frac{1}{3}$ cup crushed peppermint candies into vanilla ice cream before assembling. Roll ends of sandwiches in additional crushed peppermint candies to coat.

Tip: If the ice cream is too hard to scoop easily, microwave on HIGH 10 seconds to soften.

butterscotch blondies

1 (18.25-ounce) package yellow cake mix with pudding in the mix

⅓ cup butter or margarine, softened

3 eggs, divided

1 cup chopped pecans, toasted

1 cup (6 ounces) butterscotch-flavored chips

1 (14-ounce) can EAGLE BRAND® Sweetened Condensed Milk
(NOT evaporated milk)

1 teaspoon vanilla extract

1. Preheat oven to 350°F. In large bowl, beat cake mix, butter and 1 egg with electric mixer at medium speed until crumbly.

2. Press evenly into greased 13×9-inch baking pan. Bake 15 minutes. Remove from oven; sprinkle with pecans and butterscotch chips.

3. In small bowl, beat EAGLE BRAND®, remaining 2 eggs and vanilla. Pour evenly over chips.

4. Bake 25 to 30 minutes longer or until center is set. Cool completely. Cut into bars. Store leftovers covered at room temperature.

Makes 2 to 3 dozen bars

chocolate and oat toffee bars

¾ cup (1½ sticks) plus 2 tablespoons butter, softened, divided
1 package (about 18 ounces) yellow cake mix with pudding in the mix
2 cups uncooked quick oats
¼ cup packed brown sugar
1 egg
½ teaspoon vanilla
1 cup toffee baking bits
½ cup chopped pecans
⅓ cup semisweet chocolate chips

1. Preheat oven to 350°F. Grease 13×9-inch baking pan.

2. Beat ¾ cup butter in large bowl with electric mixer until creamy. Add cake mix, oats, brown sugar, egg and vanilla; beat 1 minute or until well blended. Stir in toffee bits and pecans. Pat dough into prepared pan.

3. Bake 31 to 35 minutes or until golden brown. Cool completely in pan on wire rack.

4. Melt remaining 2 tablespoons butter and chocolate chips in small saucepan over low heat. Drizzle warm glaze over bars. Let glaze set 1 hour at room temperature. Cut into bars. *Makes 2½ dozen bars*

ooey-gooey caramel peanut butter bars

1 package (about 18 ounces) yellow cake mix *without* pudding
   in the mix
1 cup uncooked quick oats
$^2/_3$ cup creamy peanut butter
1 egg, slightly beaten
2 tablespoons milk
1 package (8 ounces) cream cheese, softened
1 jar (12$^1/_4$ ounces) caramel ice cream topping
1 cup semisweet chocolate chips

1. Preheat oven to 350°F. Lightly grease 13×9-inch baking pan.

2. Combine cake mix and oats in large bowl. Cut in peanut butter
with pastry blender or two knives until mixture is crumbly.

3. Blend egg and milk in small bowl. Add to peanut butter mixture; stir
just until combined. Reserve 1½ cups mixture. Press remaining peanut
butter mixture into prepared pan.

4. Beat cream cheese in small bowl with electric mixer at medium speed
until fluffy. Add caramel topping; beat just until combined. Carefully spread
over peanut butter layer in pan. Break up reserved peanut butter mixture
into small pieces; sprinkle over cream cheese layer. Sprinkle with chocolate
chips.

5. Bake about 30 minutes or until nearly set in center. Cool completely
in pan on wire rack.   *Makes about 2½ dozen bars*

pecan date bars

Crust

⅓ cup shortening plus additional for greasing
1 package DUNCAN HINES® Moist Deluxe® Classic White Cake Mix
1 egg

Topping

1 package (8 ounces) chopped dates
1¼ cups chopped pecans
1 cup water
½ teaspoon vanilla extract
Confectioners' sugar

1. Preheat oven to 350°F. Grease and flour 13×9-inch baking pan.

2. For crust, cut ⅓ cup shortening into cake mix with pastry blender or 2 knives until mixture resembles coarse crumbs. Add egg; stir well. (Mixture will be crumbly.) Press mixture into bottom of prepared pan.

3. For topping, combine dates, pecans and water in medium saucepan. Bring to a boil. Reduce heat; simmer until mixture thickens, stirring constantly. Remove from heat. Stir in vanilla extract. Spread date mixture evenly over crust. Bake at 350°F for 25 to 30 minutes. Cool completely. Dust with confectioners' sugar.

Makes about 32 bars

lemon cheese bars

1 package (about 18 ounces) white or yellow cake mix with pudding in the mix

2 eggs

⅓ cup vegetable oil

1 package (8 ounces) cream cheese, softened

⅓ cup sugar

1 teaspoon lemon juice

1. Preheat oven to 350°F.

2. Combine cake mix, 1 egg and oil in large bowl; stir until crumbly. Reserve 1 cup crumb mixture. Press remaining crumb mixture into ungreased 13×9-inch baking pan. Bake 15 minutes or until light golden brown.

3. Beat remaining egg, cream cheese, sugar and lemon juice in medium bowl with electric mixer at medium speed until smooth and well blended. Spread over baked crust. Sprinkle with reserved crumb mixture.

4. Bake 15 minutes or until cream cheese layer is just set. Cool in pan on wire rack. Cut into bars. *Makes 2½ dozen bars*

To soften cream cheese quickly, remove it from the wrapper and place it on a microwavable plate. Microwave on MEDIUM (50%) 15 to 20 seconds or until slightly softened.

Cool Kid Stuff

miss pinky the pig cupcakes

2 jars (10 ounces each) maraschino cherries, well drained
1 package (about 18 ounces) white cake mix *without* pudding
   in the mix
1 cup sour cream
½ cup vegetable oil
3 egg whites
¼ cup water
½ teaspoon almond extract
   Red food coloring
1 container (16 ounces) cream cheese frosting
48 small gumdrops
   Mini candy-coated chocolate pieces, mini chocolate chips, white
     decorating icing and red sugar

1. Preheat oven to 350°F. Line 24 standard (2½-inch) muffin cups with paper baking cups. Spray 24 mini (1¾-inch) muffin cups with nonstick cooking spray. Pat cherries dry with paper towels. Place in food processor; process 4 to 5 seconds or until finely chopped.

2. Beat cake mix, sour cream, oil, egg whites, water and almond extract in large bowl with electric mixer at low speed about 1 minute or until blended. Increase speed to medium; beat 1 to 2 minutes or until smooth. Stir in cherries.

3. Spoon about 2 slightly rounded tablespoons batter into each prepared standard muffin cup, filling about half full. (Cups will be slightly less full than normal.) Spoon remaining batter into prepared mini muffin cups, filling each about one-third full.

4. Bake standard cupcakes 14 to 18 minutes and mini cupcakes 7 to 9 minutes or until toothpick inserted into centers comes out clean. Cool cupcakes in pans 5 minutes. Remove from pans; cool completely on wire racks.

5. Add food coloring to frosting, a few drops at a time, until desired shade of pink is reached. Frost tops of standard cupcakes. Press top of mini cupcake onto one side of each standard cupcake top. Frost mini cupcakes.

6. Place gumdrops between two layers of waxed paper. Flatten to ⅛-inch thickness with rolling pin; cut out triangles. Arrange triangles on cupcakes for ears; decorate faces with candy-coated chocolate pieces, chocolate chips, white icing and colored sugar.   *Makes 24 cupcakes*

flapjack party stack

1 package (about 18 ounces) yellow cake mix, plus ingredients to prepare mix
1 container (16 ounces) vanilla frosting
1 quart fresh strawberries, washed, hulled and sliced
1 cup caramel or butterscotch ice cream topping

1. Preheat oven to 350°F. Grease bottoms and sides of four 9-inch round cake pans; line pans with waxed paper.

2. Prepare and bake cake mix according to package directions. Cool cake layers in pans 15 minutes. Remove from pans; cool completely on wire racks.

3. Reserve ¼ cup frosting. Place one cake layer on serving plate; spread or pipe one third of remaining frosting in swirls on cake to resemble whipped butter. Top with sliced strawberries. Repeat with next two cake layers, frosting and strawberries. Top stack with remaining cake layer.

4. Warm caramel topping in microwave just until pourable. Drizzle over cake. Spread or pipe remaining frosting in center; garnish with remaining strawberries.   *Makes 12 servings*

slinky the snake

2 packages (about 18 ounces each) cake mix, any flavor, plus
    ingredients to prepare mix
2 containers (16 ounces each) white frosting
    Green food coloring
1 cup semisweet chocolate chips
    Red fruit roll-up
    Assorted candies

1. Prepare and bake cake mixes according to package directions for
12-cup bundt cakes. Cool completely.

2. Cut each bundt cake in half. Position each half end to end to form one
long serpentine shape as shown in photo, attaching pieces with small
amount of frosting.

3. Tint frosting with food coloring to desired shade of green. Frost entire
length of cake with green frosting, spreading frosting about halfway down
sides of cake.

4. Place chocolate chips in small resealable food storage bag. Microwave
on HIGH 20 seconds. Knead bag several times; microwave at 10-second
intervals until chocolate is melted. Cut off tiny corner of bag; pipe diamond
pattern on back of snake.

5. Cut out tongue from fruit roll-up. Decorate face and back of snake with
assorted candies. *Makes 32 to 36 servings*

crayon craze

1 package (about 18 ounces) cake mix, any flavor, plus ingredients
    to prepare mix
2 containers (16 ounces each) white frosting
    Gold, green, red, yellow, orange and blue food coloring
4 flat-bottomed ice cream cones

1. Prepare and bake cake mix according to package directions for 13×9-inch cake. Cool completely.

2. Measure 4½ inches down long sides of cake; draw line across top of cake with toothpick to create 9×4½-inch rectangle. Using toothpick line as guide, carefully cut halfway through cake (about 1 inch). (Do *not* cut all the way through cake.)

3. Split cake horizontally from 9-inch side just to cut made at 4½-inch line. Remove 9×4½×1-inch piece of cake; discard. Round edges of 9-inch side to resemble top of crayon box.

4. Tint 1 container of frosting gold. Tint 1 cup frosting green. Divide remaining frosting into four parts (scant ¼ cup each). Tint one part red, one yellow, one orange and one blue. Frost entire cake with gold frosting. Using medium writing tip and green frosting, pipe "CRAYONS" on cake. Pipe stripes, triangles and decorative borders on crayon box.

5. Gently cut ice cream cones in half vertically with serrated knife. Frost each cone half different color (red, yellow, orange and blue). Place frosted cones on cake, just below rounded edge, to resemble crayon tips.

Makes 16 to 18 servings

doodle bug cupcakes

1 package (about 18 ounces) white cake mix *without* pudding in the mix
1 cup sour cream
3 eggs
$\frac{1}{3}$ cup vegetable oil
$\frac{1}{3}$ cup water
1 teaspoon vanilla
$1\frac{1}{2}$ cups prepared cream cheese frosting
　Red, yellow, blue and green food coloring
　Red licorice strings, cut into 2-inch pieces
　Assorted round decorating candies

1. Preheat oven to 350°F. Line 24 standard (2½-inch) muffin cups with paper baking cups.

2. Beat cake mix, sour cream, eggs, oil, water and vanilla in large bowl with electric mixer at low speed about 1 minute or until blended. Beat at medium speed 1 to 2 minutes or until smooth. Spoon batter into prepared muffin cups, filling about two-thirds full.

3. Bake about 20 minutes or until toothpick inserted into centers comes out clean. Cool cupcakes in pans 5 minutes. Remove from pans; cool completely on wire racks.

4. Divide frosting evenly among four small bowls. Add food coloring to each bowl, one drop at a time, to reach desired shades; stir each frosting until well blended. Frost tops of cupcakes.

5. Poke three small holes with toothpick, on opposite sides of each cupcake, making six holes total. Insert licorice piece into each hole for legs. Decorate tops of cupcakes with assorted candies. *Makes 24 cupcakes*

cookie pizza cake

1 package (18 ounces) refrigerated chocolate chip cookie dough
1 package (about 18 ounces) chocolate cake mix, plus ingredients
    to prepare mix
1 cup prepared vanilla frosting
½ cup peanut butter
1 to 2 tablespoons milk
1 container (16 ounces) chocolate frosting
    Chocolate peanut butter cups, chopped (optional)
    Peanut butter chips (optional)

1. Preheat oven to 350°F. Coat two 12×1-inch round pizza pans with nonstick cooking spray. Press cookie dough evenly into one pan. Bake 15 to 20 minutes or until edges are golden brown. Cool cookie in pan 20 minutes. Remove from pan; cool completely on wire rack.

2. Prepare cake mix according to package directions. Fill second pan one-fourth to half full with batter. (Reserve remaining cake batter for another use, such as cupcakes.) Bake 10 to 15 minutes or until toothpick inserted into center comes out clean. Cool cake in pan 15 minutes. Gently remove from pan; cool completely on wire rack.

3. Combine vanilla frosting and peanut butter in small bowl. Gradually stir in milk, 1 tablespoon at a time, until mixture is of spreadable consistency.

4. Place cookie on serving plate. Spread peanut butter frosting over cookie. Place cake on top of cookie, trimming cookie to match size of cake, if necessary. Frost top and side of cake with chocolate frosting. Garnish with peanut butter cups and peanut butter chips, if desired.

Makes 12 to 14 servings

meteorite mini cakes

1 package (about 18 ounces) chocolate cake mix, plus ingredients
    to prepare mix
2 containers (16 ounces each) vanilla frosting, divided
    Assorted food coloring
1 bag (11 ounces) chocolate baking chunks

1. Preheat oven to 350°F. Spray 12 standard (2½-inch) muffin cups with nonstick cooking spray.

2. Prepare cake mix according to package directions. Divide batter evenly among muffin cups. Bake 20 to 25 minutes or until toothpick inserted into centers comes out clean. Cool cupcakes in pan 5 minutes. Remove from pan; cool completely on wire rack.

3. Use kitchen shears to trim cupcake edges and form rounded, irregular shapes. Place 2 cups frosting in microwavable bowl and heat on LOW (30%) about 30 seconds or until melted. Tint as desired with food coloring. Drizzle frosting over cupcakes, coating completely.

4. Chill cakes 20 minutes. Press chocolate chunks into cakes to create bumpy surface. Melt remaining frosting and tint as desired. Drizzle over cakes to coat baking chunks with frosting. Chill until ready to serve.

Makes 12 servings

pb & j sandwich cake

1 package (about 18 ounces) white cake mix, plus ingredients
    to prepare mix
¾ cup powdered sugar
5 tablespoons peanut butter
2 to 3 tablespoons whipping cream or milk
1 tablespoon butter, softened
½ cup strawberry or grape jam

1. Preheat oven to 350°F. Grease two 8-inch square baking pans.

2. Prepare cake mix according to package directions. Spread batter evenly in prepared pans.

3. Bake 30 minutes or until toothpick inserted into centers comes out clean. Cool cake layers in pans 30 minutes. Remove from pans; cool completely on wire racks.

4. Carefully slice off browned tops of both layers to create flat, even layers. Place one layer on serving plate, cut side up.

5. Beat powdered sugar, peanut butter, 2 tablespoons cream and butter with electric mixer at medium speed until light and creamy. Add remaining 1 tablespoon cream, if necessary, to reach spreading consistency. Gently spread filling over cut side of cake layer on serving plate. Spread jam over peanut butter filling. Top with second cake layer, cut side up.

6. Cut cake in half diagonally to resemble sandwich. To serve, cut into thin slices across the diagonal using serrated knife.   *Makes 12 servings*

sherbet starburst

1 package (about 18 ounces) lemon cake mix, plus ingredients
   to prepare mix
2 quarts raspberry or mango sherbet, or any flavors
1 container (15 ounces) white pourable frosting
   Yellow food coloring
   Orange decorating sugar

1. Prepare and bake cake mix according to package directions for two
8- or 9-inch round cake layers. Cool cake layers completely.

2. Scoop sherbet into small bowl. Freeze until ready to serve.

3. Cut one cake layer into 8 wedges. (Reserve remaining cake layer for
another use.) Place cake wedges on wire rack set over waxed paper-lined
baking sheet to catch drips.

4. Blend frosting and food coloring in large microwavable bowl until desired
shade of yellow is reached. Microwave frosting on HIGH 20 seconds; stir.
Pour frosting slowly over each cake wedge, making sure to cover all sides.
Sprinkle with sugar. Let stand about 20 minutes or until set.

5. When ready to serve, arrange cakes wedges in circle with tips pointing
out. Place dish of sherbet in center.   *Makes 8 servings*

colossal birthday cupcake

1 package (about 18 ounces) devil's food cake mix, plus ingredients
    to prepare mix
1 container (16 ounces) vanilla or chocolate frosting, divided
¼ cup peanut butter
    Construction paper or aluminum foil
    Fruit-flavored candy wafers or chocolate shavings

1. Preheat oven to 350°F. Grease and flour two 8-inch round cake pans.

2. Prepare cake mix according to package directions. Spread batter evenly in prepared pans. Bake about 30 minutes or until toothpick inserted into centers comes out clean. Cool cake layers completely.

3. Blend ¾ cup frosting and peanut butter in medium bowl. Place one cake layer on serving plate; spread evenly with peanut butter frosting. Top with second cake layer; spread top with remaining vanilla frosting, mounding frosting slightly higher in center.

4. Cut 36×3½-inch piece of construction paper; pleat paper every ½ inch. Wrap around side of cake to resemble baking cup. Arrange candy wafers decoratively on frosting.

Makes 12 servings

touchdown!

1 package (about 18 ounces) cake mix, any flavor, plus ingredients
    to prepare mix
2 cups prepared white frosting
  Green food coloring
  Assorted color decorating gels
1 square (2 ounces) almond bark
2 pretzel rods
4 thin pretzel sticks
  Small bear-shaped graham cookies

1. Prepare and bake cake mix according to package directions for
13×9-inch cake. Cool completely.

2. Tint frosting with food coloring to desired shade of green. Frost entire
cake with green frosting. Pipe field lines with white decorating gel.

3. Melt almond bark in tall glass according to package directions. Break
off one fourth of each pretzel rod; discard shorter pieces. Break 2 pretzel
sticks in half. Dip pretzels in melted almond bark, turning to coat completely
and tapping off excess. Using pretzel rods for support posts, pretzel sticks
for crossbars and pretzel stick halves for uprights, arrange pretzels in two
goalpost formations on waxed paper; let stand until set. Carefully peel
waxed paper from goalposts; arrange on each end of cake.

4. Meanwhile, decorate bear-shaped cookies with decorating gels; arrange
cookies on cake as desired. *Makes 16 to 20 servings*

big purple purse

1 package (about 18 ounces) cake mix, any flavor, plus ingredients
    to prepare mix
1 container (16 ounces) white frosting
  Red and blue food coloring
2 red licorice pull-apart twists
1 white chocolate-coated pretzel
  Round sugar-covered colored candies
  Candy lipstick, necklace and ring (optional)
  Chocolate coins (optional)

1. Prepare and bake cake mix according to package directions in two
9-inch round cake pans. Cool cake layers in pans 10 minutes. Remove
from pans; cool completely on wire racks. Reserve one cake layer for
another use.

2. Blend frosting, 4 drops red food coloring and 4 drops blue food coloring
in medium bowl. Add additional food coloring, one drop at a time, until
desired shade of purple is reached.

3. Spread about ½ cup frosting over top of cake layer. Cut in half; press
frosted sides together to form half circle. Place cake, cut side down, on
serving plate.

4. Spread frosting over top and sides of cake. Press licorice twists into top
of cake to form purse handles. Add pretzel for clasp. Gently press round
candies into sides of cake. Arrange candy lipstick, necklace, ring and coins
around cake, if desired.   *Makes 8 to 10 servings*

pupcakes

1 package (about 18 ounces) chocolate cake mix, plus ingredients to prepare mix
½ cup (1 stick) butter, softened
4 cups powdered sugar
¼ to ½ cup half-and-half or milk
Red and yellow fruit roll-ups
Candy-coated chocolate pieces
Assorted colored jelly beans

1. Preheat oven to 350°F. Line 24 standard (2½-inch) muffin cups with paper baking cups.

2. Prepare cake mix and bake in prepared pans according to package directions. Cool cupcakes in pans 15 minutes. Remove from pans; cool completely on wire racks.

3. Beat butter in large bowl with electric mixer until creamy. Gradually add powdered sugar to form very stiff frosting, scraping down side of bowl occasionally. Gradually add half-and-half until frosting is of desired consistency. Frost tops of cupcakes.

4. Cut out ear and tongue shapes from fruit roll-ups with scissors; arrange on cupcakes, pressing into frosting. Add chocolate pieces and jelly beans to create eyes and noses. *Makes 24 cupcakes*

ladybug

1 package (about 18 ounces) white cake mix, plus ingredients
    to prepare mix
1 container (16 ounces) vanilla frosting
¼ cup red raspberry preserves
    Red decorating sugar
    Candy-coated chocolate pieces
8 dark chocolate discs or mint chocolate cookies
    String licorice and assorted gumdrops
    Large peppermint patty
1 cup flaked coconut tinted green with food coloring

1. Prepare and bake cake mix according to package directions for two 9-inch round cake layers. Cool cake layers completely.

2. Place one cake layer on serving plate; spread with frosting. Spread raspberry preserves over frosting to within ½ inch of edge. Top with second cake layer; frost top and side of cake with remaining frosting.

3. Sprinkle top of cake with sugar. Decorate with chocolate pieces and discs as shown in photo. Create ladybug face with string licorice and assorted gumdrops; attach to mint patty with small amounts of frosting. Place mint patty on cake. Press coconut onto side of cake.

Makes 12 servings

pizza cake

1 package (about 18 ounces) yellow cake mix, plus ingredients
    to prepare mix
1 container (16 ounces) white frosting
  Red food coloring
  Orange round gummy candies
  Green sugar-coated sour gummy strips, cut into small pieces
  Purple round sour gummy rings
  White candy-coated licorice strips

1. Preheat oven to 350°F. Grease and flour 12-inch deep-dish pizza pan.

2. Prepare cake mix according to package directions. Pour batter into prepared pan.

3. Bake 18 to 25 minutes or until toothpick inserted into center comes out clean. Cool cake in pan about 15 minutes. Remove from pan; cool completely on wire rack.

4. Blend frosting and food coloring in medium bowl until desired shade of red is reached. Place cake on serving plate; frost top of cake to within ¼ inch of edge.

5. Arrange candies over cake to resemble pizza toppings and cheese.

Makes 12 servings

Fun &
Fruity

crunchy peach snack cake

1 package (9 ounces) yellow cake mix
1 container (6 ounces) peach yogurt
1 egg
¼ cup peach fruit spread
¾ cup square whole grain oat cereal with cinnamon, slightly crushed
  Whipped cream (optional)

1. Place rack in center of oven; preheat oven to 350°F. Lightly grease 8-inch square baking pan.

2. Beat cake mix, yogurt and egg in medium bowl with electric mixer at low speed about 1 minute or until blended. Beat at medium speed 1 to 2 minutes or until smooth.

3. Spread batter in prepared pan. Drop fruit spread by ½ teaspoonfuls over cake batter. Sprinkle with cereal.

4. Bake 25 minutes or until toothpick inserted into center of cake comes out clean. Cool on wire rack. Serve with whipped cream.

Makes 9 servings

double berry layer cake

1 package DUNCAN HINES® Moist Deluxe® Strawberry Supreme
  Cake Mix
⅔ cup strawberry jam
2½ cups fresh blueberries, rinsed, drained
1 container (8 ounces) frozen whipped topping, thawed
  Fresh strawberry slices for garnish

1. Preheat oven to 350°F. Grease and flour two 9-inch round cake pans.

2. Prepare, bake and cool cakes following package directions for basic recipe.

3. Place one cake layer on serving plate. Spread with ⅓ cup strawberry jam. Arrange 1 cup blueberries on jam. Spread half the whipped topping to within ½ inch of cake edge. Place second cake layer on top. Repeat with remaining ⅓ cup strawberry jam, 1 cup blueberries and remaining whipped topping. Garnish with strawberry slices and remaining ½ cup blueberries. Refrigerate until ready to serve.   *Makes 12 servings*

Tip: For best results, cut cake with serrated knife; clean knife after each slice.

blueberry cream cheese pound cake

1 package (16 ounces) pound cake mix, divided
1½ cups fresh blueberries
4 ounces cream cheese, softened
2 eggs
¾ cup milk
    Powdered sugar (optional)

1. Preheat oven to 350°F. Grease 9×5-inch loaf pan.

2. Place ¼ cup cake mix in medium bowl; add blueberries and toss until well coated.

3. Beat cream cheese in large bowl with electric mixer at medium speed 1 minute or until light and fluffy. Add eggs, one at a time, beating well after each addition.

4. Add remaining cake mix alternately with milk, beginning and ending with cake mix, beating well after each addition. Beat 1 minute at medium speed or until light and fluffy. Fold blueberry mixture into batter. Pour batter into prepared pan.

5. Bake 55 to 60 minutes or until toothpick inserted into center comes out clean. Cool cake in pan 10 minutes. Remove from pan; cool completely on wire rack. Lightly sprinkle with powdered sugar, if desired.

Makes 12 servings

Fun & Fruity

cran-lemon coffee cake

1 package (about 18 ounces) yellow cake mix with pudding in the mix
1 cup water
3 eggs
$\frac{1}{3}$ cup butter, melted and cooled
$\frac{1}{4}$ cup fresh lemon juice
1 tablespoon grated lemon peel
$1\frac{1}{2}$ cups coarsely chopped cranberries
    Lemon Glaze (recipe follows)
    Additional grated lemon peel (optional)

1. Preheat oven to 350°F. Grease and flour 12-inch bundt or tube pan.

2. Beat cake mix, water, eggs, butter, lemon juice and 1 tablespoon lemon peel in large bowl with electric mixer at low speed 2 minutes. Fold in cranberries. Spread batter evenly in prepared pan.

3. Bake about 55 minutes or until toothpick inserted near center comes out clean. Cool in pan 10 minutes. Remove from pan; cool completely on wire rack.

4. Prepare Lemon Glaze; drizzle over coffee cake. Garnish with grated lemon peel. Serve warm or at room temperature.　　*Makes 12 servings*

Lemon Glaze: Beat 1 cup powdered sugar and 3 tablespoons fresh lemon juice in small bowl until well blended.

Variation: For mini coffee cakes, grease and flour 9 (1-cup) mini bundt pan cups. Prepare batter as directed above; fill prepared cups almost two-thirds full. Bake 18 to 20 minutes or until toothpick inserted near centers comes out clean. Glaze and garnish as directed above.

fresh fruit tart

1 package (about 18 ounces) butter recipe yellow cake mix
½ cup (1 stick) butter, melted and cooled
2 eggs
1 teaspoon vanilla
⅓ cup apricot jam
1½ cups whipped topping
2 cups sliced strawberries
1 kiwifruit, peeled and sliced
⅓ cup fresh blueberries

1. Preheat oven to 350°F. Spray 10-inch springform pan with nonstick cooking spray.

2. Beat cake mix, butter, eggs and vanilla in large bowl with electric mixer at low speed 2 minutes. (Batter will be very thick.) Pour batter into prepared pan. Spray fingers with cooking spray and pat down top of batter to flatten slightly.

3. Bake 25 to 30 minutes or until center is firm and toothpick inserted into center comes out clean. Cool completely in pan on wire rack. Remove side of pan; slide cake onto serving platter.

4. Heat apricot jam in small microwavable bowl on HIGH 30 seconds or until jam is thin and syrupy.

5. Spread whipped topping evenly over crust. Arrange fruit decoratively over topping. Brush fruit with melted jam. Refrigerate leftovers.

Makes 10 servings

apple spice custard cake

1 (18.25- or 18.5-ounce) package spice cake mix

2 medium apples, peeled, cored and chopped

1 (14-ounce) can EAGLE BRAND® Sweetened Condensed Milk
(NOT evaporated milk)

1 (8-ounce) container sour cream

¼ cup lemon juice

Ground cinnamon (optional)

1. Preheat oven to 350°F. Grease and flour 13×9-inch baking pan. Prepare cake mix according to package directions.

2. Stir in apples. Pour batter into prepared pan. Bake 30 to 35 minutes or until toothpick inserted near center comes out clean.

3. In medium bowl, combine EAGLE BRAND® and sour cream; mix well. Stir in lemon juice. Remove cake from oven; spread sour cream mixture evenly over hot cake.

4. Return to oven; bake 5 minutes or until set. Sprinkle with cinnamon (optional). Cool. Chill. Store leftovers covered in refrigerator.

Makes 12 servings

pineapple almond coffee cake

1 can (8 ounces) crushed pineapple in juice, undrained

1 teaspoon cornstarch

1 tablespoon grated orange peel

1 package (9 ounces) golden yellow cake mix

$\frac{1}{3}$ cup water

1 egg

$\frac{1}{2}$ cup sliced almonds

1 tablespoon powdered sugar

1. Preheat oven to 350°F. Spray 9-inch springform pan with nonstick cooking spray.

2. Combine pineapple with juice and cornstarch in small saucepan; stir until smooth. Bring to a boil over medium-high heat; continue to boil 1 minute, stirring frequently. Remove from heat; stir in orange peel. Set aside to cool slightly.

3. Beat cake mix, water and egg in medium bowl with electric mixer at low speed 1 minute or until blended. Increase speed to medium; beat 1 to 2 minutes or until smooth. Pour half of batter into prepared pan. Spoon pineapple mixture evenly over batter. *Do not stir.* Gently spoon remaining batter evenly over pineapple mixture. Sprinkle with almonds.

4. Bake 30 minutes or until cake is golden and springs back when lightly pressed with fingertips. Remove to wire rack; cool completely. Remove side of pan; slide cake onto serving platter. Sprinkle with powdered sugar. Cut into wedges. *Makes 10 servings*

Note: This cake will be puffy when it is removed from the oven, but will fall slightly upon cooling. The pineapple will settle to the bottom, making a slightly moist base.

flower power strawberry cake

1 package (about 18 ounces) white cake mix *without* pudding
    in the mix
2 containers (6 ounces each) strawberry yogurt
4 eggs
$\frac{1}{3}$ cup vegetable oil
1 package (4-serving size) strawberry gelatin
1 container (8 ounces) thawed frozen whipped topping, divided
13 medium strawberries
    Yellow food coloring

1. Preheat oven to 350°F. Lightly grease 13×9-inch baking pan.

2. Beat cake mix, yogurt, eggs, oil and gelatin in large bowl with electric mixer at low speed about 1 minute or until blended. Increase speed to medium; beat 1 to 2 minutes or until smooth. Spread batter evenly in prepared pan.

3. Bake 38 to 43 minutes or until toothpick inserted into center comes out clean. Cool completely in pan on wire rack.

4. Reserve $\frac{1}{2}$ cup whipped topping. Spread remaining topping over cooled cake; score into 15 (3×2½-inch) rectangles. Cut each strawberry lengthwise into 6 wedges. Place 5 strawberry wedges in each rectangle on cake, pointed ends towards center, making flower as shown in photo.

5. Tint reserved whipped topping with yellow food coloring; place in resealable food storage bag. Cut off $\frac{1}{8}$ inch from corner of bag. Pipe dot into center of each flower. Serve cake immediately or loosely cover and refrigerate for up to 24 hours. *Makes 15 servings*

berry cobbler cake

2 cups (1 pint) fresh or frozen berries (blueberries, blackberries and/or raspberries)
1 package (9 ounces) yellow cake mix
1 teaspoon ground cinnamon
1 egg
1 cup water, divided
¼ cup sugar
1 tablespoon cornstarch
Ice cream (optional)

1. Preheat oven to 375°F.

2. Place berries in 9-inch square baking pan; set aside.

3. Combine cake mix and cinnamon in large bowl. Add egg and ¼ cup water; stir until well blended. Spoon over berries.

4. Combine sugar and cornstarch in small bowl. Stir in remaining ¾ cup water until sugar mixture dissolves; pour over cake batter and berries.

5. Bake 40 to 45 minutes or until lightly browned. Serve warm or at room temperature with ice cream, if desired. *Makes 6 servings*

apple-walnut glazed spice baby cakes

1 package (about 18 ounces) spice cake mix
1⅓ cups plus 3 tablespoons water, divided
3 eggs
⅓ cup vegetable oil
½ teaspoon vanilla
¾ cup chopped walnuts
12 ounces Granny Smith apples, peeled and cut into ½-inch cubes
(about 3 medium)
¼ teaspoon ground cinnamon
1 jar (12 ounces) caramel ice cream topping

1. Preheat oven to 350°F. Grease and flour 12 small (1-cup) bundt pan cups.

2. Beat cake mix, 1⅓ cups water, eggs, oil and vanilla in large bowl with electric mixer at low speed 30 seconds. Beat at medium speed 2 minutes. Spoon batter evenly into prepared cups.

3. Bake 25 minutes or until toothpick inserted near centers comes out clean. Cool cakes in pans 15 minutes. Carefully invert cakes onto wire racks; cool completely.

4. Meanwhile, place large skillet over medium-high heat. Add walnuts; cook and stir 3 minutes or until lightly browned. Transfer to small bowl. Combine apples, remaining 3 tablespoons water and cinnamon in same skillet; cook and stir over medium-high heat 3 minutes or until apples are crisp-tender. Remove from heat; stir in walnuts and caramel topping. Spoon glaze over cakes.

Makes 12 cakes

topsy-turvy banana crunch cake

⅓ cup uncooked old-fashioned oats
3 tablespoons packed brown sugar
1 tablespoon all-purpose flour
¼ teaspoon ground cinnamon
2 tablespoons butter
2 tablespoons chopped pecans
1 package (9 ounces) yellow cake mix
½ cup sour cream
½ cup mashed banana (about 1 medium)
1 egg, slightly beaten

1. Preheat oven to 350°F. Lightly grease 8-inch square baking pan.

2. Combine oats, brown sugar, flour and cinnamon in small bowl. Cut in butter with pastry blender or two knives until crumbly. Stir in pecans.

3. Beat cake mix, sour cream, banana and egg in medium bowl with electric mixer at low speed about 1 minute or until blended. Beat at medium speed 1 to 2 minutes or until smooth. Spoon half of batter into prepared pan; sprinkle with half of oat topping. Top with remaining batter and topping.

4. Bake 25 to 30 minutes or until toothpick inserted into center comes out clean. Cool completely in pan on wire rack.   *Makes 9 servings*

tropical sunshine cake

1 package (18.25 ounces) yellow cake mix
1 can (12 fluid ounces) NESTLÉ® CARNATION® Evaporated Milk
2 large eggs
1 can (20 ounces) crushed pineapple in juice, drained (juice reserved),
    divided
½ cup chopped almonds
¾ cup sifted powdered sugar
1 cup flaked coconut, toasted
    Whipped cream

PREHEAT oven to 350°F. Grease 13×9-inch baking pan.

COMBINE cake mix, evaporated milk and eggs in large mixer bowl. Beat on low speed for 2 minutes. Stir in *1 cup* pineapple. Pour batter into prepared baking pan. Sprinkle with almonds.

BAKE for 30 to 35 minutes or until wooden pick inserted in center comes out clean. Cool in pan on wire rack for 15 minutes.

COMBINE sugar and 2 tablespoons *reserved* pineapple juice in small bowl; mix until smooth. Spread over warm cake; sprinkle with coconut and *remaining* pineapple. Cool completely before serving. Top with whipped cream.

Makes 12 servings

mandarin orange tea cake

1 package (16 ounces) pound cake mix
½ cup plus 2 tablespoons orange juice, divided
2 eggs
¼ cup milk
1 can (15 ounces) mandarin orange segments in light syrup, drained
¾ cup powdered sugar
   Grated peel of 1 orange

1. Preheat oven to 350°F. Grease 9-inch bundt pan.

2. Beat cake mix, ½ cup orange juice, eggs and milk in large bowl with electric mixer at medium speed 2 minutes or until light and fluffy. Fold in orange segments. Pour batter into prepared pan.

3. Bake 45 minutes or until golden brown and toothpick inserted near center comes out clean. Cool in pan 15 minutes. Invert cake onto wire rack; cool completely.

4. Combine sugar, orange peel and remaining 2 tablespoons orange juice in small bowl; stir until smooth. Drizzle glaze over cake. Allow glaze to set about 5 minutes before serving. *Makes 16 servings*

strawberry stripe refrigerator cake

Cake

  1 package **DUNCAN HINES®** Moist Deluxe® Classic White Cake Mix

  2 packages (10 ounces) frozen sweetened strawberry slices, thawed

Topping

  1 package (4-serving size) vanilla-flavor instant pudding and
     pie filling mix

  1 cup milk

  1 cup whipping cream, whipped

  Fresh strawberries for garnish (optional)

1. Preheat oven to 350°F. Grease and flour 13×9×2-inch pan.

2. For cake, prepare, bake and cool following package directions. Poke holes 1 inch apart in top of cake using handle of wooden spoon. Purée thawed strawberries with juice in blender or food processor. Spoon evenly over top of cake, allowing mixture to soak into holes.

3. For topping, combine pudding mix and milk in large bowl. Stir until smooth. Fold in whipped cream. Spread over cake. Decorate with fresh strawberries, if desired. Refrigerate at least 4 hours.

Makes 12 to 16 servings

Variation: **For a Neapolitan Refrigerator Cake, substitute Duncan Hines® Moist Deluxe® Devil's Food Cake Mix for White Cake Mix and follow directions listed above.**

easy apple butter cake

1 package (about 18 ounces) yellow cake mix *without* pudding
    in the mix
1 package (4-serving size) vanilla instant pudding mix
4 eggs
1 cup sour cream
1 cup apple butter
½ cup apple juice
¼ cup vegetable oil
1 teaspoon ground cinnamon
½ teaspoon ground nutmeg
½ teaspoon ground cloves
¼ teaspoon salt
    Powdered sugar (optional)

1. Preheat oven to 375°F. Spray 10-inch tube pan with nonstick cooking spray.

2. Beat cake mix, pudding mix, eggs, sour cream, apple butter, apple juice, oil, cinnamon, nutmeg, cloves and salt in large bowl with electric mixer at low speed 1 minute. Beat at medium speed 2 minutes or until well blended and fluffy. Pour batter into prepared pan.

3. Bake 45 to 50 minutes or until toothpick inserted near center comes out clean. Cool cake in pan 20 minutes. Run sharp knife along edge of pan to release cake from pan; invert cake onto serving plate. Cool completely.

4. Just before serving, place 9-inch paper doily over cake; sift powdered sugar over doily. Carefully remove doily. *Makes 12 servings*

caribbean cake squares

1 package (9 ounces) yellow cake mix
2 egg whites
½ cup orange juice
2 cans (8 ounces each) crushed pineapple in juice
 Additional orange juice
1 tablespoon cornstarch
½ cup slivered almonds
½ cup flaked coconut
2 large ripe bananas
1 can (15 ounces) mandarin oranges, drained

1. Preheat oven to 350°F. Spray 13×9-inch nonstick baking pan with nonstick cooking spray.

2. Beat cake mix, egg whites and orange juice in medium bowl with electric mixer at medium speed 2 minutes or until well blended. Spoon batter evenly into prepared pan.

3. Bake 11 to 12 minutes or until toothpick inserted into center comes out clean. Cool completely in pan on wire rack.

4. Drain pineapple juice into 2-cup measure; add additional orange juice to measure 1½ cups liquid. Stir in cornstarch until smooth. Pour juice mixture into medium saucepan. Bring to a boil over high heat, stirring constantly. Boil 1 minute, stirring constantly. Remove from heat.

5. Place almonds and coconut in large skillet; heat over medium heat until almonds and coconut are golden brown, stirring frequently.

6. Spread pineapple evenly over cake. Slice bananas and arrange over pineapple. Top with mandarin oranges. Carefully drizzle juice mixture evenly over fruit. Sprinkle with almond mixture. Cover and refrigerate 1 to 4 hours. *Makes 16 servings*

Chocolate
Obsession

tortoise snack cake

1 package (about 18 ounces) devil's food cake mix, plus ingredients
    to prepare mix
1 cup chopped pecans
1 cup semisweet chocolate chips
½ teaspoon vanilla
½ cup caramel sauce
    Additional caramel sauce and chopped pecans (optional)

1. Preheat oven to 350°F. Grease 13×9-inch baking pan.

2. Prepare cake mix according to package directions; stir pecans,
chocolate chips and vanilla into batter. Pour into prepared pan. Drizzle
½ cup caramel sauce over batter; swirl caramel into batter with knife.

3. Bake 32 minutes or until cake begins to pull away from sides of pan
and toothpick inserted into center comes out clean. Cool slightly in pan
on wire rack. Top each serving with additional caramel sauce and pecans.

Makes 24 servings

double chocolate chewies

1 package DUNCAN HINES® Moist Deluxe® Butter Recipe Fudge
    Cake Mix
2 eggs
½ cup (1 stick) butter or margarine, melted
1 package (6 ounces) semisweet chocolate chips
1 cup chopped nuts
    Confectioners' sugar (optional)

1. Preheat oven to 350°F. Grease bottom only of 13×9×2-inch baking pan.

2. Combine cake mix, eggs and melted butter in large bowl. Stir until
thoroughly blended. (Mixture will be stiff.) Stir in chocolate chips and nuts.

Press mixture evenly into prepared pan. Bake at 350°F for 25 to 30 minutes or until toothpick inserted in center comes out clean. *Do not overbake.* Cool completely. Cut into bars. Dust with confectioners' sugar, if desired.

Makes 36 bars

Tip: For a special effect, cut a paper towel into ¼-inch-wide strips. Place strips in diagonal pattern on top of cooled bars before cutting. Place confectioners' sugar in tea strainer. Tap strainer lightly to dust surface with sugar. Carefully remove strips.

double chocolate bundt cake

1 package (about 18 ounces) chocolate cake mix *without* pudding
   in the mix
1 package (4-serving size) chocolate instant pudding mix
4 eggs, beaten
¾ cup water
¾ cup sour cream
½ cup oil
6 ounces (1 cup) semisweet chocolate chips
   Powdered sugar

1. Preheat oven to 350°F. Spray 10-inch bundt or tube pan with nonstick cooking spray.

2. Beat cake mix, pudding mix, eggs, water, sour cream and oil in large bowl with electric mixer at medium speed until well blended. Stir in chocolate chips; pour into prepared pan.

3. Bake 55 to 60 minutes or until cake springs back when lightly touched. Cool cake 1 hour in pan. Invert cake onto serving plate; cool completely. Sprinkle with powdered sugar before serving.

Makes 10 to 12 servings

chocolate gingersnaps

¾ cup sugar

1 package (about 18 ounces) chocolate cake mix *without* pudding
   in the mix

1 tablespoon ground ginger

2 eggs

⅓ cup vegetable oil

1. Preheat oven to 350°F. Spray cookie sheets with nonstick cooking spray. Place sugar in shallow bowl.

2. Combine cake mix and ginger in large bowl. Add eggs and oil; stir until well blended. Shape tablespoonfuls of dough into 1-inch balls; roll in sugar to coat. Place 2 inches apart on prepared cookie sheets.

3. Bake about 10 minutes. Remove cookies to wire racks; cool completely.

Makes about 3 dozen cookies

Purchase ground ginger in small amounts, as it will begin to lose its flavor after four to six months. Like other spices, it should be stored in an airtight container in a cool, dry place.

white chocolate lovers' layer cake

12 squares (1 ounce each) white chocolate, divided
1 cup (2 sticks) butter, softened, divided
1 package (about 18 ounces) white cake mix
1 cup milk
3 eggs
1½ teaspoons vanilla, divided
6 ounces cream cheese, softened
   Dash salt
1½ cups powdered sugar
¼ cup seedless raspberry jam
1 cup fresh raspberries (optional)

1. Preheat oven to 350°F. Grease and flour two 9-inch round cake pans. Microwave 6 squares white chocolate and ½ cup butter in microwavable bowl on MEDIUM-HIGH (70%) 1½ minutes; stir. If necessary, microwave at additional 10- to 15-second intervals, stirring just until chocolate is melted. Cool slightly.

2. Beat cake mix, milk, eggs, ¾ teaspoon vanilla and white chocolate mixture in large bowl with electric mixer at low speed 1 minute. Beat at medium speed 2 minutes or until well blended. Pour into prepared pans.

3. Bake about 25 minutes or until toothpick inserted into centers comes out clean. Cool cake layers in pans 10 minutes. Remove from pans; cool completely on wire racks.

4. Melt remaining 6 squares white chocolate; cool slightly. Beat remaining ½ cup butter and cream cheese in medium bowl with electric mixer until well blended. Beat in melted chocolate, remaining ¾ teaspoon vanilla and salt. Add powdered sugar; beat until frosting is light and fluffy.

5. Place one cake layer on serving plate. Top with frosting; spread jam evenly over frosting. Place second cake layer over jam. Frost top and side of cake with remaining frosting. Garnish with raspberries. *Makes 12 servings*

triple chocolate pb minis

2 packages (4.4 ounces each) chocolate peanut butter cups*
1 package (about 18 ounces) chocolate fudge cake mix, plus
    ingredients to prepare mix
¾ cup whipping cream
1½ cup semisweet chocolate chips

*Refrigerate candy to make chopping easier.

1. Preheat oven to 350°F. Line 60 mini (1¾-inch) muffin cups with paper baking cups. Finely chop peanut butter cups; refrigerate candy while preparing batter.

2. Prepare cake mix according to package directions; stir 1 cup chopped candy into batter. Spoon batter into prepared muffin cups, filling two-thirds full.

3. Bake about 9 minutes or until toothpick inserted into centers comes out clean. Cool cupcakes in pans 5 minutes. Remove from pans; cool completely on wire racks.

4. Meanwhile, heat cream to a boil. Place chocolate chips in medium heatproof bowl; pour cream over chips. Let stand 5 minutes; stir until blended and smooth. Glaze will thicken as it cools (or refrigerate glaze to thicken more quickly).

5. Dip tops of cooled cupcakes in chocolate glaze; sprinkle with remaining chopped candy.   *Makes 60 mini cupcakes*

hot fudge sundae cake

1 package DUNCAN HINES® Moist Deluxe® Dark Chocolate Fudge
   Cake Mix
½ gallon brick vanilla ice cream

Fudge Sauce
   1 can (12 ounces) evaporated milk
1¼ cups sugar
   4 squares (1 ounce each) unsweetened chocolate
  ¼ cup (½ stick) butter or margarine
1½ teaspoons vanilla extract
  ¼ teaspoon salt
   Whipped cream and maraschino cherries for garnish

1. Preheat oven to 350°F. Grease and flour 13×9×2-inch pan. Prepare,
bake and cool cake following package directions.

2. Remove cake from pan. Split cake in half horizontally. Place bottom
layer back in pan. Cut ice cream into even slices and place evenly over
bottom cake layer (use all the ice cream). Place remaining cake layer
over ice cream. Cover and freeze.

3. For fudge sauce, combine evaporated milk and sugar in medium
saucepan. Cook, stirring constantly, over medium heat until mixture
comes to a rolling boil. Boil and stir for 1 minute. Add unsweetened
chocolate and stir until melted. Beat over medium heat until smooth.
Remove from heat. Stir in butter, vanilla extract and salt.

4. Cut cake into squares. For each serving, place cake square on
plate; spoon hot fudge sauce on top. Garnish with whipped cream
and maraschino cherry. *Makes 12 to 16 servings*

Tip: Fudge sauce may be prepared ahead and refrigerated in tightly sealed
jar. Reheat when ready to serve.

polka dot cake

1 package (about 18 ounces) chocolate cake mix, plus ingredients
    to prepare mix
¾ cup white chocolate chips
2 bars (3½ ounces each) good-quality bittersweet or semisweet
    chocolate, broken into small pieces
¼ cup (½ stick) butter, cut into small chunks
¼ cup whipping cream
1 tablespoon powdered sugar
    Dash salt
¼ cup small chocolate nonpareil candies

1. Preheat oven to 350°F. Generously spray 12-cup bundt pan with nonstick cooking spray.

2. Prepare cake mix according to package directions. Pour batter into prepared pan; sprinkle with chocolate chips.

3. Bake 40 minutes or until toothpick inserted near center comes out clean. Cool cake in pan 30 minutes. Invert onto wire rack; cool completely. Place sheet of waxed paper under wire rack.

4. Combine chocolate pieces, butter, cream, powdered sugar and salt in small heavy saucepan. Heat over low heat, stirring constantly, just until butter and chocolate melt. Mixture should be tepid, not hot. Immediately spoon chocolate glaze over cake, spreading to cover side as well as top. Scoop up any glaze from waxed paper and spoon over cake.

5. Arrange nonpareil candies over glaze. Let glaze set about 2 hours at room temperature. Do not refrigerate. *Makes 16 servings*

devil's food pancakes

1 package (about 18 ounces) devil's food cake mix
2 cups milk
2 eggs
½ cup mini chocolate chips
   Powdered sugar
   Strawberry Glaze (recipe follows, optional)

1. Whisk cake mix, milk and eggs in large bowl until well blended. Stir in chocolate chips.

2. Heat griddle or large nonstick skillet over medium-low to medium heat (350°F*). Pour ¼ cup batter onto griddle for each pancake. Cook 3 to 4 minutes or until edges appear dry; turn and cook 2 to 3 minutes. Repeat with remaining batter.

3. Sprinkle with powdered sugar and serve with Strawberry Glaze.

Makes about 22 (4-inch) pancakes

Do not cook pancakes at a higher temperature as they burn easily.

Strawberry Glaze: Combine 1 cup chopped fresh strawberries and ⅓ cup strawberry preserves in medium bowl.

Note: These pancakes freeze well. Freeze four pancakes in one resealable sandwich bag. Reheat in the microwave.

Chocolate Obsession

double chocolate chip snack cake

1 package (about 18 ounces) devil's food cake mix with pudding
    in the mix, divided
2 eggs
½ cup water
¼ cup vegetable oil
½ teaspoon cinnamon
1 cup semisweet chocolate chips, divided
¼ cup packed brown sugar
2 tablespoons butter, melted
¾ cup white chocolate chips

1. Preheat oven to 350°F. Grease 9-inch round cake pan.

2. Reserve ¾ cup cake mix. Beat remaining cake mix, eggs, water, oil and cinnamon in large bowl with electric mixer at medium speed 2 minutes. Remove ½ cup batter; reserve for another use.* Spread remaining batter in prepared pan; sprinkle with ½ cup semisweet chocolate chips.

3. Combine reserved cake mix and brown sugar in medium bowl. Stir in butter and remaining ½ cup semisweet chocolate chips; mix well. Sprinkle mixture over batter in pan.

4. Bake 35 to 40 minutes or until toothpick inserted into center comes out clean and cake springs back when lightly touched. Cool cake in pan 10 minutes. Remove from pan; cool completely on wire rack.

5. Place white chocolate chips in resealable food storage bag; seal bag. Microwave on HIGH 10 seconds and knead bag gently. Repeat until chips are melted. Cut off ¼ inch from corner of bag; drizzle chocolate over cake. Let glaze set before cutting cake into wedges.

Makes 8 to 10 servings

If desired, extra batter can be used for cupcakes: Pour batter into two foil baking cups placed on baking sheet; bake at 350°F 20 to 25 minutes or until toothpick inserted into centers comes out clean.

chocolate dream torte

1 package DUNCAN HINES® Moist Deluxe® Dark Chocolate Fudge Cake Mix
1 (6-ounce) package semisweet chocolate chips, melted
1 (8-ounce) container frozen non-dairy whipped topping, thawed
1 container DUNCAN HINES® Creamy Home-Style Milk Chocolate Frosting
3 tablespoons finely chopped dry roasted pistachios

1. Preheat oven to 350°F. Grease and flour two 9-inch round cake pans.

2. Prepare, bake and cool cake as directed on package for basic recipe.

3. For chocolate hearts garnish, spread melted chocolate to ⅛-inch thickness on waxed paper-lined baking sheet. Cut shapes with heart cookie cutter when chocolate begins to set. Refrigerate until firm. Push out heart shapes. Set aside.

4. To assemble, split each cake layer in half horizontally. Place one split cake layer on serving plate. Spread one third of whipped topping on top. Repeat with remaining layers and whipped topping, leaving top plain. Frost side and top with frosting. Sprinkle pistachios on top. Position chocolate hearts by pushing points down into cake. Refrigerate until ready to serve.

Makes 12 to 16 servings

Chocolate Strawberry Dream Torte: Omit semisweet chocolate chips and chopped pistachios. Proceed as directed through step 2. Fold 1½ cups chopped fresh strawberries into whipped topping in large bowl. Assemble as directed, filling torte with strawberry mixture and frosting with Milk Chocolate frosting. Garnish cake with strawberry fans and mint leaves, if desired.

chocolate crispy treat cake

1 package (about 18 ounces) chocolate fudge cake mix, plus
 ingredients to prepare mix
1 cup semisweet chocolate chips
¼ cup light corn syrup
¼ cup (½ stick) butter
½ cup powdered sugar
2 cups crisp rice cereal
4 cups mini marshmallows (half of 10½-ounce package)

1. Preheat oven to 350°F. Grease bottom only of 13×9-inch pan.

2. Prepare cake mix according to package directions; pour into prepared pan. Bake 28 minutes or until cake is almost done.

3. Meanwhile, heat chocolate chips, corn syrup and butter in medium saucepan over low heat, stirring frequently, until chocolate and butter are melted. Remove from heat; stir in powdered sugar. Gently stir in cereal until well blended.

4. Remove cake from oven; sprinkle marshmallows over top of cake in single layer. Return cake to oven; bake 2 to 3 minutes longer until marshmallows puff up slightly.

5. Spread chocolate cereal mixture over marshmallows. Let cake stand until set.   *Makes 24 servings*

Note: This cake is best within a day or two of baking; after two days the cereal becomes soggy.

chocolate hazelnut cookies

$\frac{1}{2}$ cup chopped pecans
1 package (8 ounces) cream cheese, softened
$\frac{1}{2}$ cup (1 stick) butter, softened
1 egg
1 package (about 18 ounces) devil's food cake mix
1 jar (12 ounces) chocolate hazelnut spread
$\frac{1}{4}$ cup powdered sugar

1. Preheat oven 350°F. Place pecans in small resealable bag. Finely crush pecans with meat mallet or rolling pin. Place in small skillet over medium high heat; toast pecans 1$\frac{1}{2}$ minutes or until browned, stirring constantly. Remove from heat and set aside.

2. Beat cream cheese and butter in medium bowl with electric mixer at low speed 30 seconds or until smooth. Add egg; beat at medium speed until well blended. Add cake mix; beat at low speed 2 minutes until mixture is smooth and resembles thick cookie dough. Stir in pecans.

3. Shape dough into 1-inch balls; spray palms lightly with cooking spray, if necessary, to make handling easier. Place 1 inch apart on ungreased cookie sheets.

4. Bake 8 minutes. (Cookies will appear underbaked.) Cool cookies on cookie sheets 5 minutes. Remove to wire racks to cool completely.

5. Spoon 1 teaspoon chocolate hazelnut spread over each cookie; sprinkle with powdered sugar. *Makes 4 dozen cookies*

fudgy mocha cupcakes with chocolate coffee ganache

1 package (about 18 ounces) devil's food cake mix *without* pudding in the mix

1 package (4-serving size) chocolate fudge instant pudding and pie filling mix

1⅓ cups strongly brewed coffee, cooled to room temperature

3 eggs

½ cup vegetable oil

6 ounces semisweet chocolate, finely chopped

½ cup whipping cream

2 teaspoons instant coffee granules

½ cup white frosting

1. Preheat oven to 350°F. Line 18 standard (2½-inch) muffin cups with paper baking cups.

2. Beat cake mix, pudding mix, coffee, eggs and oil in large bowl with electric mixer at medium speed 2 minutes or until well blended. Spoon batter into prepared muffin cups, filling two-thirds full.

3. Bake 22 to 24 minutes or until toothpick inserted into centers comes out clean. Cool cupcakes in pans 10 minutes. Remove from pans; cool completely on wire racks.

4. For ganache, place chocolate in small bowl. Heat cream and instant coffee in small saucepan over medium-low heat until bubbles appear around edge of pan. Pour cream over chocolate; let stand about 2 minutes. Stir until mixture is smooth and shiny. Allow ganache to cool completely. (It will be slightly runny.)

5. Dip tops of cupcakes into chocolate ganache; smooth surface.

6. Place frosting in pastry bag fitted with small round writing tip. Pipe desired letters onto cupcakes. *Makes 18 cupcakes*

chocolate petits fours

1 package DUNCAN HINES® Moist Deluxe® Dark Chocolate Fudge
   Cake Mix
1 package (7 ounces) pure almond paste
½ cup seedless red raspberry jam
3 cups semisweet chocolate chips
½ cup vegetable shortening plus additional for greasing

1. Preheat oven to 350°F. Grease and flour 13×9×2-inch pan.

2. Prepare, bake and cool cake following package directions for basic recipe. Remove from pan. Cover and store overnight (see Tip on page 212). Level top of cake. Trim ¼-inch strip of cake from all sides. (Be careful to make straight cuts.) Cut cake into small squares, rectangles or triangles with serrated knife. Cut round and heart shapes with 1½- to 2-inch cookie cutters. Split each individual cake horizontally into two layers.

3. For filling, cut almond paste in half. Roll half the paste between two sheets of waxed paper to ⅛-inch thickness. Cut into same shapes as individual cakes. Repeat with second half of paste. Warm jam in small saucepan over low heat until thin. Remove top of one cake. Spread ¼ to ½ teaspoon jam on inside of each cut surface. Place one almond paste cutout on bottom layer. Top with second half of cake, jam side down. Repeat with remaining cakes.

4. For glaze, place chocolate chips and ½ cup shortening in 4-cup glass measuring cup. Microwave at MEDIUM (50% power) for 2 minutes; stir. Microwave for 2 minutes longer at MEDIUM; stir until smooth. Place 3 assembled cakes on cooling rack over bowl. Spoon chocolate glaze over each cake until top and sides are completely covered. Remove to waxed paper when glaze has stopped dripping. Repeat process until all cakes are covered. (Return chocolate glaze in bowl to glass measuring cup as needed; microwave at MEDIUM for 30 to 60 seconds to thin.)

continued on page 212

5. Place remaining chocolate glaze in resealable plastic bag; seal. Place bag in bowl of hot water for several minutes. Dry with paper towel. Knead until chocolate is smooth. Snip pinpoint hole in bottom corner of bag. Drizzle or decorate top of each petit four. Let stand until chocolate is set. Store in single layer in airtight containers. *Makes 24 to 32 servings*

Tip: To make cutting the cake into shapes easier, bake the cake one day before assembling.

chocolate peanut butter candy bars

1 package (about 18 ounces) devil's food or dark chocolate cake mix
    without pudding in the mix
1 can (5 ounces) evaporated milk
⅓ cup butter, melted
½ cup dry-roasted peanuts
4 packages (1½ ounces each) chocolate peanut butter cups,
    coarsely chopped

1. Preheat oven to 350°F. Lightly grease 13×9-inch baking pan.

2. Beat cake mix, evaporated milk and butter in large bowl with electric mixer at medium speed until well blended. (Dough will be stiff.) Spread two thirds of dough in prepared pan. Sprinkle with peanuts.

3. Bake 10 minutes; remove from oven and sprinkle with chopped candy.

4. Drop remaining dough by large spoonfuls over candy. Bake 15 to 20 minutes or until set. Cool completely in pan on wire rack.

Makes 2 dozen bars

Holiday

Treats

chocolate sweetheart cupcakes

1 package (about 18 ounces) dark chocolate cake mix, plus
   ingredients to prepare mix
1 container (16 ounces) vanilla frosting
3 tablespoons seedless raspberry jam
   Powdered sugar (optional)

1. Preheat oven to 350°F. Line 24 standard (2½-inch) muffin cups with paper baking cups.

2. Prepare cake mix according to package directions. Spoon batter into prepared muffin cups, filling two-thirds full.

3. Bake about 18 minutes or until toothpick inserted into centers comes out clean. Cool cupcakes in pans 10 minutes. Remove from pans; cool completely on wire racks.

4. Blend frosting and jam in medium bowl until smooth. Cut off rounded tops of cupcakes with serrated knife. Cut out heart shape from each cupcake top with mini cookie cutter.

5. Spread frosting mixture generously over cupcake bottoms, mounding slightly in center. Replace cupcake tops, pressing gently to fill cutout hearts with frosting mixture. Sprinkle with powdered sugar, if desired.

Makes 24 cupcakes

i think you're "marbleous" cupcakes

1 package (about 18 ounces) cake mix, any flavor, with pudding
 in the mix
1¼ cups water
3 eggs
¼ cup vegetable oil
1 container (16 ounces) vanilla frosting
1 tube (4¼ ounces) red decorating icing

1. Preheat oven to 350°F. Line 24 standard (2½-inch) muffin cups with paper baking cups or spray with nonstick cooking spray.

2. Prepare cake mix according to package directions with water, eggs and oil. Spoon batter into prepared muffin cups, filling two-thirds full.

3. Bake 20 to 25 minutes or until toothpick inserted into centers comes out clean. Cool cupcakes in pans 20 minutes. Remove from pans; cool completely on wire racks.

4. Spread 1½ to 2 tablespoons frosting over each cupcake. Fit round decorating tip onto tube of icing. Squeeze 5 dots of icing over each cupcake. Swirl toothpick through icing and frosting in continuous motion to make marbleized pattern or heart shapes. *Makes 24 cupcakes*

Holiday Treats

pretty-in-pink peppermint cupcakes

1 package (about 18 ounces) white cake mix
1⅓ cups water
3 egg whites
2 tablespoons vegetable oil or melted butter
½ teaspoon peppermint extract
3 to 4 drops red liquid food coloring *or* ¼ teaspoon gel food coloring
1 container (16 ounces) prepared vanilla frosting
½ cup crushed peppermint candies (about 16 candies)

1. Preheat oven to 350°F. Line 30 standard (2½-inch) muffin cups with paper baking cups.

2. Beat cake mix, water, egg whites, oil, peppermint extract and food coloring in large bowl with electric mixer at low speed 30 seconds. Beat at medium speed 2 minutes. Spoon batter into prepared muffin cups, filling three-fourths full.

3. Bake 20 to 22 minutes or until toothpick inserted into centers comes out clean. Cool cupcakes in pans 10 minutes. Remove from pans; cool completely on wire racks. (At this point, cupcakes may be frozen up to 3 months. Thaw at room temperature before frosting.)

4. Spread frosting over cooled cupcakes; sprinkle with crushed candies. Store at room temperature up to 24 hours or cover and refrigerate up to 3 days before serving.   *Makes 30 cupcakes*

green's lucky cake

1 package (18.25 ounces) any flavor cake mix, plus ingredients
    to prepare mix
$\frac{1}{2}$ teaspoon water
2 to 3 drops green food coloring
$\frac{1}{2}$ cup sweetened shredded coconut
6 tablespoons butter, softened
$3\frac{3}{4}$ cups powdered sugar, divided
3 to 4 tablespoons milk
$\frac{1}{2}$ teaspoon vanilla extract
Blue food coloring
1 cup "M&M's"® Chocolate Mini Baking Bits

Prepare and bake cake as directed on package for 13×9-inch cake. Cool
cake completely on wire rack. In small bowl combine water and food
coloring. Add coconut and stir until evenly tinted; set aside. In large bowl
cream butter until light. Add 2 cups powdered sugar; beat until fluffy. Blend
in 3 tablespoons milk and vanilla. Beat in remaining 1¾ cups powdered
sugar until frosting is smooth. Add additional milk, 1 teaspoon at a time, if
necessary to make frosting spreadable. Tint frosting desired shade of blue.
Frost cake and decorate with tinted coconut and "M&M's"® Chocolate Mini
Baking Bits as shown in photo.   *Makes 16 to 20 servings*

kelly green mini bundt cakes

2 tablespoons butter, melted
1 package (about 18 ounces) white cake mix, plus ingredients
    to prepare mix
  Green food coloring
1 container (16 ounces) white frosting
  Green decorating sugar

1. Preheat oven to 350°F. Brush 12 mini (1-cup) bundt pan cups with butter.

2. Prepare cake mix according to package directions. Add food coloring to batter, one drop at a time, until desired shade of green is reached. Fill prepared bundt pan cups half full.

3. Bake 20 minutes or until toothpick inserted near centers comes out clean. Cool cakes in pans 5 minutes. Carefully place wire rack on top of pans; invert pans. Lightly tap bottom of pans to help release cakes. Cool completely on wire racks.

4. Place frosting in small microwavable bowl. Add food coloring, one drop at a time, until desired shade of green is reached. Microwave on LOW (30%) for 30 seconds or until pourable but not melted. Spoon frosting over tops of cakes. Sprinkle with green sugar. *Makes 12 mini cakes*

leprechaun cupcakes

**1 package (about 18 ounces) yellow or white cake mix,
plus ingredients to prepare mix
1 container (16 ounces) vanilla frosting
Green, orange and red gumdrops, black decorating gel
and small candies**

1. Preheat oven to 350°F. Line 24 standard (2½-inch) muffin cups with paper baking cups.

2. Prepare cake mix according to package directions. Spoon batter into prepared muffin cups, filling two-thirds full.

3. Bake 15 to 20 minutes or until toothpick inserted into centers comes out clean. Cool cupcakes in pans 10 minutes. Remove from pans; cool completely on wire racks. Frost cooled cupcakes with vanilla frosting.

4. Roll out green gumdrops on generously sugared surface. Cut out pieces to resemble hats. Pipe gel onto hats for hatbands; place candies on hatbands for buckles. Place hats on cupcakes. Roll out orange gumdrops on generously sugared surface. Cut out pieces to resemble sideburns and beards; place on cupcakes. Roll out red gumdrops on generously sugared surface. Cut out small pieces to resemble mouths; place on cupcakes. Place candies on cupcakes for eyes. *Makes 24 cupcakes*

liberty's torches

26 flat-bottomed ice cream cones
1 package (about 18 ounces) cake mix, any flavor, plus ingredients
   to prepare mix
Yellow food coloring
1 container (16 ounces) white frosting
26 red, yellow and orange fruit roll-ups

1. Preheat oven to 350°F. Stand 24 ice cream cones in 13×9-inch pan and remaining 2 cones in muffin cups or small loaf pan. (Or, place all cones in muffin cups.)

2. Prepare cake mix according to package directions. Fill each cone with 2½ tablespoons batter (filling to within about ¼ inch of top of cone base).

3. Bake 30 minutes or until cake tops spring back when lightly touched and toothpick inserted into centers comes out clean. Remove cones to wire racks; cool completely.

4. Stir 4 to 5 drops food coloring into frosting to reach desired shade of yellow. Frost cupcakes. Cut flames from fruit roll-ups using kitchen shears or sharp knife. Fold or roll flames to stand upright; arrange on cupcakes before frosting sets.   *Makes 26 cupcakes*

spider cupcakes

1 package (about 18 ounces) yellow or white cake mix
1 cup solid-pack pumpkin
¾ cup water
3 eggs
2 tablespoons vegetable oil
1 teaspoon ground cinnamon
1 teaspoon pumpkin pie spice*
  Orange food coloring
1 container (16 ounces) vanilla, cream cheese or caramel frosting
4 squares (1 ounce each) semisweet chocolate
48 black gumdrops

*Or substitute ½ teaspoon ground cinnamon, ¼ teaspoon ground ginger and ⅛ teaspoon each ground allspice and ground nutmeg for the pumpkin pie spice.

1. Preheat oven to 350°F. Line 24 standard (2½-inch) muffin cups with paper baking cups or spray with nonstick cooking spray.

2. Beat cake mix, pumpkin, water, eggs, oil, cinnamon and pumpkin pie spice in large bowl with electric mixer at medium speed 3 minutes or until well blended. Spoon ¼ cup batter into each muffin cup. Bake about 20 minutes or until toothpick inserted into centers comes out clean. Cool cupcakes in pans 10 minutes. Remove from pans; cool completely on wire racks.

3. Add food coloring to frosting until desired shade of orange is reached. Frost cupcakes.

4. Place chocolate in small resealable food storage bag. Microwave on MEDIUM (50%) 40 seconds. Knead bag; microwave 30 seconds to 1 minute or until chocolate is melted and smooth. Cut off tiny corner of bag. Drizzle chocolate in four or five concentric circles over top of cupcakes. Immediately draw 6 to 8 lines at regular intervals from center to edges of cupcakes with toothpick or knife to create web.

continued on page 230

5. For spiders, place one gumdrop in center of web. Roll out another gumdrop with rolling pin on generously sugared surface. Slice thinly and roll into "legs." Arrange legs around gumdrop to form spiders.

Makes 24 cupcakes

deadly diamonds

1 package (9 ounces) devil's food cake mix, plus ingredients
    to prepare mix
1 cup marshmallow creme
$\frac{1}{4}$ cup red currant jelly

1. Prepare and bake cake mix according to package directions in 9-inch square baking pan. Cool cake in pan 15 minutes. Remove from pan; cool completely on wire rack.

2. Cut cake into 4 strips. Trim edges; cut each strip on diagonal to form 4 diamonds (total of 16 diamonds).

3. Just before serving, spread 1 tablespoon marshmallow creme over each diamond. Place jelly in microwavable bowl; microwave on LOW (30%) 20 to 30 seconds. Stir until melted. Drizzle about $\frac{1}{2}$ teaspoon jelly over each diamond; swirl into marshmallow surface to create dripping effect. Serve immediately.

Makes 16 servings

squished and squirmy sandwiches

1 package (9 ounces) vanilla confetti cake mix
2 eggs
⅓ cup vegetable oil
1 quart vanilla ice cream
32 gummy worms

1. Preheat oven to 375°F.

2. Mix cake mix, eggs and oil in large bowl with spoon until well moistened. Shape dough into 32 (1¼-inch) balls. Place 2 inches apart on ungreased cookie sheets. Gently flatten dough to ¼-inch thickness.

3. Bake 6 to 8 minutes or until edges are light golden brown. Cool cookies 1 minute on cookie sheets; remove to wire racks to cool completely.

4. Working quickly, place 2 tablespoons ice cream on flat side of one cookie and top with gummy worm, allowing worm to stick out as much as possible. Top with 2 tablespoons ice cream and another worm. Top with another cookie, flat side down, pressing down to flatten slightly. Wrap in foil and freeze. Repeat with remaining cookies, ice cream and gummy worms. *Makes 16 sandwiches*

When shaping the dough, try to create cookies that are uniform in size and shape so they finish baking at the same time. For even baking and browning of cookies, bake them in the center of the oven. If the heat distribution in your oven is uneven, turn the cookie sheet halfway through the baking time.

scaredy cat cake

1 package (about 18 ounces) devil's food cake mix, plus ingredients
    to prepare mix
1 container (16 ounces) dark chocolate fudge frosting
4 individual square chocolate snack cakes
1 large orange or pink gumdrop
  Granulated sugar
  Black decorating gel
  Black string licorice, cut into $3\frac{1}{2}$- to 4-inch lengths
2 large yellow gumdrops

1. Prepare and bake cake mix according to package directions in two 8-inch round cake pans. Cool in pans 15 minutes. Remove from pans; cool completely on wire racks.

2. Place one cake layer upside down on serving platter; spread with chocolate frosting. Top with second cake layer, top side up. Frost top and side of cake.

3. Cut snack cakes in half diagonally. Frost tops of all snack cake triangles. Make 2 stacks of 4 triangles each. Place at top of round cake for ears; frost to blend in with round cake. Use back of spoon to pull frosting on side of cake out into points to resemble fur.

4. Roll out orange gumdrop with rolling pin on generously sugared surface. Cut out large triangle; place in center of cake for nose. Use decorating gel to create mouth and licorice for whiskers.

5. Roll out yellow gumdrops with rolling pin on generously sugared surface. Cut out pointed ovals; place on cake for eyes. Pipe gel onto eyes.

Makes 12 servings

boo hands cupcakes

1 package (about 18 ounces) cake mix, any flavor, plus ingredients
   to prepare mix
1 container (16 ounces) white frosting
36 large marshmallows
24 black jelly beans, halved
12 orange jelly beans, halved

1. Preheat oven to 350°F. Line 24 standard (2½-inch) muffin cups with paper baking cups or spray with nonstick cooking spray.

2. Prepare cake mix according to package directions. Spoon batter evenly into prepared muffin cups.

3. Bake 15 to 20 minutes or until toothpick inserted into centers comes out clean. Cool cupcakes in pans on wire racks 15 minutes. Remove from pans; cool completely on wire racks.

4. Spread small amount of frosting on cupcakes. Cut 12 marshmallows in half crosswise; place one half on each cupcake. Frost cupcakes again, completely covering marshmallow half.

5. Roll each remaining marshmallow between hands to about 2½ inches in length. Cut in half and arrange on either side of cupcake to create hands; cover completely with frosting. Create faces using 2 black jelly bean halves for eyes and orange jelly bean half for nose. *Makes 24 cupcakes*

pumpkin cheesecake bars

1 (16-ounce) package pound cake mix
3 eggs, divided
2 tablespoons butter or margarine, melted
4 teaspoons pumpkin pie spice, divided
1 (8-ounce) package cream cheese, softened
1 (14-ounce) can EAGLE BRAND® Sweetened Condensed Milk
    (NOT evaporated milk)
1 (15-ounce) can pumpkin (2 cups)
$\frac{1}{2}$ teaspoon salt
1 cup chopped nuts

1. Preheat oven to 350°F. In large bowl, on low speed, combine cake mix, 1 egg, butter and 2 teaspoons pumpkin pie spice until crumbly. Press onto bottom of ungreased 15×10-inch jellyroll pan.

2. In large bowl, beat cream cheese until fluffy. Gradually beat in EAGLE BRAND® until smooth. Beat in remaining 2 eggs, pumpkin, remaining 2 teaspoons pumpkin pie spice and salt; mix well.

3. Pour into prepared crust; sprinkle with nuts.

4. Bake 30 to 35 minutes or until set. Cool. Chill; cut into bars. Store leftovers covered in refrigerator.

Makes 4 dozen bars

reindeer cupcakes

1 package (about 18 ounces) chocolate cake mix, plus ingredients
    to prepare mix

$\frac{1}{4}$ cup ($\frac{1}{2}$ stick) butter, softened

4 cups powdered sugar

5 to 6 tablespoons brewed espresso

$\frac{1}{2}$ cup (3 ounces) semisweet chocolate chips, melted

1 teaspoon vanilla

   Dash salt

24 pretzel twists, broken in half

   Assorted candies

1. Preheat oven to 350°F. Line 24 standard (2½-inch) muffin cups with paper baking cups.

2. Prepare cake mix according to package directions. Spoon batter into prepared muffin cups, filling two-thirds full.

3. Bake 15 to 20 minutes or until toothpick inserted into centers comes out clean. Cool cupcakes in pans 10 minutes. Remove from pans; cool completely on wire racks.

4. Beat butter in large bowl with electric mixer at medium speed until creamy. Gradually add powdered sugar and 4 tablespoons espresso; beat until smooth. Add melted chocolate, vanilla and salt; beat until well blended. Add remaining espresso, 1 tablespoon at a time, until frosting is of desired spreading consistency.

5. Frost cooled cupcakes. Decorate with broken pretzel pieces for antlers and assorted candies for faces. *Makes 24 cupcakes*

easy eggnog pound cake

1 (18.25-ounce) package yellow cake mix
1 (4-serving size) package instant vanilla pudding and pie filling mix
¾ cup BORDEN® EggNog
¾ cup vegetable oil
4 eggs
½ teaspoon ground nutmeg
Confectioners' sugar (optional)

1. Preheat oven to 350°F. In large bowl, combine cake mix, pudding mix, BORDEN® EggNog and oil; beat on low speed until moistened. Add eggs and nutmeg; beat at medium-high speed 4 minutes.

2. Pour into greased and floured 10-inch fluted or tube pan. Bake 40 to 45 minutes or until toothpick inserted near center comes out clean. Cool 10 minutes; remove from pan. Cool completely. Sprinkle with confectioners' sugar (optional). *Makes one (10-inch) cake*

Prep Time: **10 minutes**
Bake Time: **40 to 45 minutes**

When using a bundt or tube pan, be sure to generously grease the center tube and fluted sides to prevent the cake from sticking.

snowman cupcakes

1 package (about 18 ounces) yellow or white cake mix,
   plus ingredients to prepare mix
2 containers (16 ounces each) vanilla frosting
4 cups flaked coconut
15 large marshmallows
15 miniature chocolate covered peanut butter cups
   Small red candies
   Pretzel sticks
   Green and red decorating gels

1. Preheat oven to 350°F. Grease 15 standard (2½-inch) muffin cups
and 15 mini (1¾-inch) muffin cups.

2. Prepare cake mix according to package directions. Spoon batter into
prepared muffin cups, filling two-thirds full.

3. Bake 10 to 15 minutes for mini cupcakes and 15 to 20 minutes for
standard cupcakes or until golden and toothpick inserted into centers
comes out clean. Cool cupcakes in pans 10 minutes. Remove from
pans; cool completely on wire racks.

4. To assemble, frost bottoms and sides of large cupcakes; coat with
coconut. Repeat with mini cupcakes. Attach mini cupcakes to large
cupcakes with frosting to form snowman bodies. Attach marshmallows
to mini cupcakes with frosting to form heads. Attach inverted peanut
butter cups to marshmallows with frosting to form hats. Use pretzels
for arms and red candies for buttons as shown in photo. Pipe faces
with decorating gels. *Makes 15 snowmen*

holiday thumbprint cookies

1 package (9 ounces) yellow cake mix
3 tablespoons orange juice
2 teaspoons grated orange peel
$\frac{1}{2}$ teaspoon vanilla
5 teaspoons strawberry fruit spread
2 tablespoons pecans, chopped

1. Preheat oven to 350°F. Spray cookie sheets with nonstick cooking spray.

2. Beat cake mix, orange juice, orange peel and vanilla in medium bowl with electric mixer at medium speed 2 minutes or until mixture is crumbly. Beat at medium-high speed 2 minutes or until smooth dough forms. (Dough will be very sticky.)

3. Coat hands with nonstick cooking spray. Shape dough into 1-inch balls. Place balls 2$\frac{1}{2}$ inches apart on prepared cookie sheets. Press center of each ball with thumb. Fill each thumbprint with $\frac{1}{4}$ teaspoon fruit spread. Sprinkle with pecans.

4. Bake 8 to 9 minutes or until cookies are light golden brown and no longer shiny. Remove to wire racks to cool completely.

Makes 20 cookies

Acknowledgments

The publisher would like to thank the companies listed below for the use of their recipes and photographs in this publication.

Dole Food Company, Inc.

Duncan Hines® and Moist Deluxe® are registered trademarks of Pinnacle Foods Corp.

EAGLE BRAND®

The Hershey Company

© Mars, Incorporated 2007

Nestlé USA

Index

METRIC CONVERSION CHART

VOLUME MEASUREMENTS (dry)

1/8 teaspoon = 0.5 mL
1/4 teaspoon = 1 mL
1/2 teaspoon = 2 mL
3/4 teaspoon = 4 mL
1 teaspoon = 5 mL
1 tablespoon = 15 mL
2 tablespoons = 30 mL
1/4 cup = 60 mL
1/3 cup = 75 mL
1/2 cup = 125 mL
2/3 cup = 150 mL
3/4 cup = 175 mL
1 cup = 250 mL
2 cups = 1 pint = 500 mL
3 cups = 750 mL
4 cups = 1 quart = 1 L

VOLUME MEASUREMENTS (fluid)

1 fluid ounce (2 tablespoons) = 30 mL
4 fluid ounces (1/2 cup) = 125 mL
8 fluid ounces (1 cup) = 250 mL
12 fluid ounces (1 1/2 cups) = 375 mL
16 fluid ounces (2 cups) = 500 mL

WEIGHTS (mass)

1/2 ounce = 15 g
1 ounce = 30 g
3 ounces = 90 g
4 ounces = 120 g
8 ounces = 225 g
10 ounces = 285 g
12 ounces = 360 g
16 ounces = 1 pound = 450 g

DIMENSIONS

1/16 inch = 2 mm
1/8 inch = 3 mm
1/4 inch = 6 mm
1/2 inch = 1.5 cm
3/4 inch = 2 cm
1 inch = 2.5 cm

OVEN TEMPERATURES

250°F = 120°C
275°F = 140°C
300°F = 150°C
325°F = 160°C
350°F = 180°C
375°F = 190°C
400°F = 200°C
425°F = 220°C
450°F = 230°C

BAKING PAN SIZES

Utensil	Size in Inches/Quarts	Metric Volume	Size in Centimeters
Baking or Cake Pan (square or rectangular)	8×8×2	2 L	20×20×5
	9×9×2	2.5 L	23×23×5
	12×8×2	3 L	30×20×5
	13×9×2	3.5 L	33×23×5
Loaf Pan	8×4×3	1.5 L	20×10×7
	9×5×3	2 L	23×13×7
Round Layer Cake Pan	8×1½	1.2 L	20×4
	9×1½	1.5 L	23×4
Pie Plate	8×1¼	750 mL	20×3
	9×1¼	1 L	23×3
Baking Dish or Casserole	1 quart	1 L	—
	1½ quart	1.5 L	—
	2 quart	2 L	—